A MEAL FOR TWO

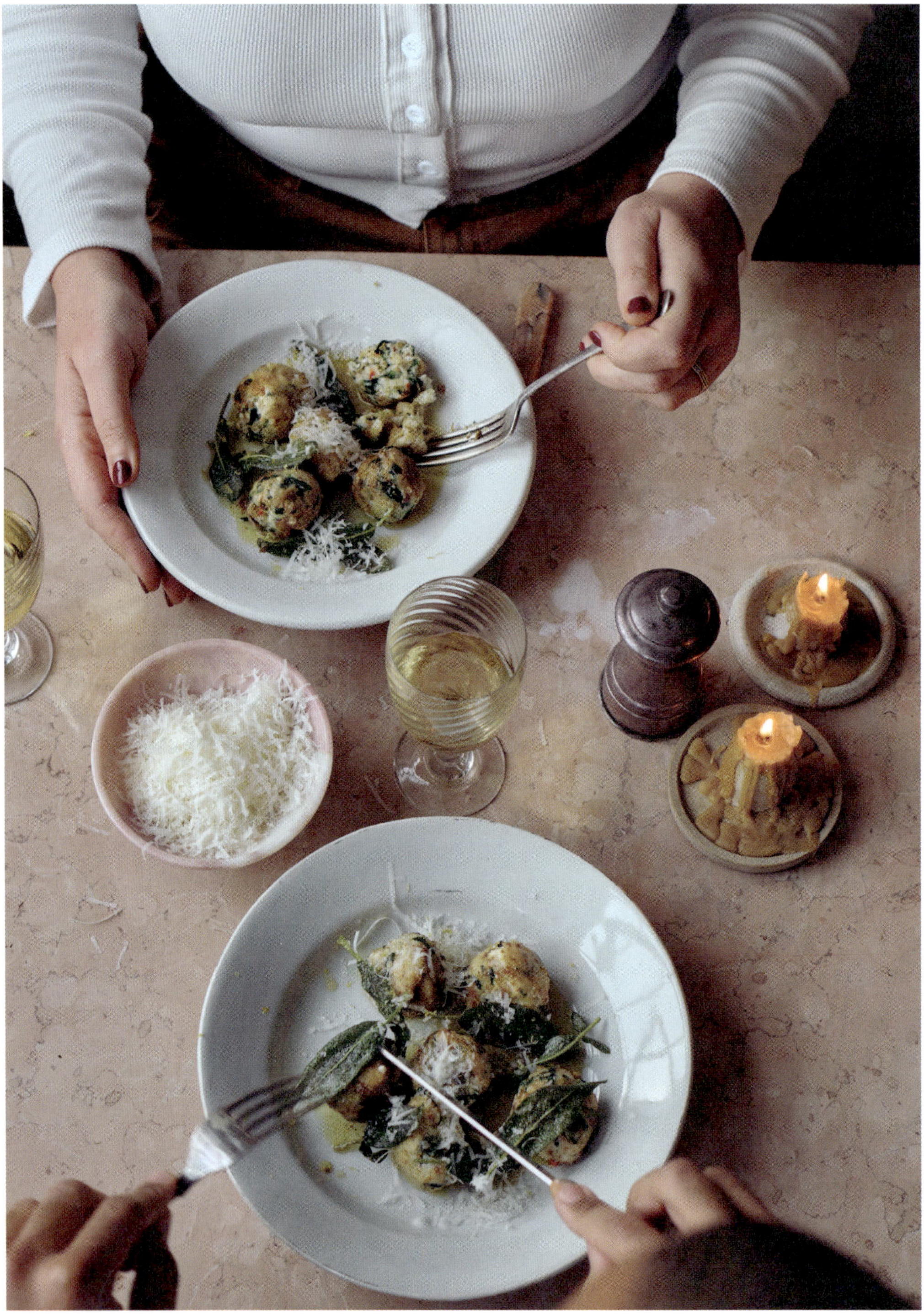

Emily Ezekiel

Photography by Issy Croker

A MEAL FOR TWO

Recipes to Treat Your Favorite People

Hardie Grant
NORTH AMERICA

CONTE

NTS

6 Introduction

10 15-Minute Meals

42 Feeding Friendships

76 Date Nights

108 Something Special for the Weekend (and the magic of leftovers)

132 Sweet Moments for Two

160 Cocktails and Dreams

176 The Art of Cocktail Snacking

Whether you are cooking for a date, a friend, or your mom, cooking for two is all about making mealtimes more enjoyable, intimate, and special.

In a world where food prices are climbing, it is the perfect time to rediscover the joy of cooking and being together. My goal with this cookbook is to help you fall in love with your kitchen again and create truly delicious moments and memories to be shared.

This book is packed with tasty, easy-to-make recipes that will always impress. You will find plenty of quick, 15-minute meals that are packed with flavor, using smart shortcuts so you can whip up something delicious, even when you're time-poor.

When you want to impress, there is a chapter on date nights to help you do just that. And for those fun weekends when you have extra time on your hands, there are impressive recipes that will help you create memorable meals. Plus, there are also some clever ideas for using up leftovers, so there's always something good waiting for you at the weekend or in the freezer.

Don't worry; I haven't forgotten the sweet moments. When you want a treat but don't want to make a huge dessert, there are easy sweets for any day of the week. To top it off, there are some fun cocktail recipes to help you turn any meal into something special.

Cooking for two should be more than just preparing food; it's all about creating memories and enjoying time with the people you care about.

INTRODUCTION 7

GUESS WHO'S COMING TO DINNER...

Whether you are planning a romantic dinner for a special person in your life, or fancy making something indulgent for your best friend, or just need a midweek inspirational meal, here are some sample menus for every occasion for a perfect meal for two.

Sizzling evening menu

Stuffed fried jalapeños *(page 186)*;
Tangerine citrustini *(page 162)*

–

Steamed whole fish finished with a sizzling scallion oil *(page 79)*

–

Miso and dark chocolate freezer cookies *(page 146)*

Pull it out of the bag in no time

Anchovies and charred bread *(page 182)*;
Vermouth spritz *(page 166)*

–

Fried lemon spaghetti *(page 25)*

–

Grated frozen nectarine with olive oil and salt over ice cream *(page 151)*

For a best friend

Stuffed queen olives with blue cheese *(page 181)*;
A perfect negroni *(page 166)*

–

My perfect Caesar *(page 44)*

–

Earl Grey chocolate pudding *(page 141)*

Fun evening in

Mackerel pâte on toast *(page 182)*;
Summer green garden *(page 172)*

–

Spicy crispy gyoza with
smashed cucumber salad *(page 125)*

–

Orange blossom and lemon granita *(page 144)*

The menu that gives you both a hug

Whipped butter and salted radishes *(page 180)*;
Dirtiest martini *(page 169)*

–

Schnitzel and kohlrabi slaw *(page 48)*

–

Almond and cherry clafoutis *(page 156)*

The date menu

Elevated potato chips *(page 178)*;
Spicy tequila picante *(page 173)*

–

Lady and the tramp spaghetti and meatballs
with a spiced tomato sauce *(page 86)*

–

My heavenly Calvados tiramisu *(page 134)*

15-
MINUTE

MEALS

Baked salmon with crispy capers and speedy green aioli

Serves: 2
Prep Time: 5 minutes
Cook Time: 10 minutes

FOR THE SALMON
2 (5 ounces / 140 g) salmon filets, skinless
2 tablespoons extra-virgin olive oil
½ lemon, thinly sliced
1 jalapeño chile, sliced
1 garlic clove, sliced
Salt

FOR THE CRISPY CAPERS
¼ cup (60 ml) light olive oil or other light oil
¼ cup (50 g) capers, drained

FOR THE AIOLI
Scant ½ cup (100 g) mayonnaise
½ ounce (15 g) parsley
½ ounce (15 g) basil
1 garlic clove, peeled but left whole
Juice of ½ lemon

FOR SERVING
¼ cup (200 g) baby leaf spinach
Juice of ½ lemon
2 lemon wedges

This baked salmon is a go-to in our house when we want a speedy, delicious meal that still impresses and is packed full of nutrients. If you are short on time, a good-quality store-bought mayonnaise is an excellent substitute for the aioli.

Preheat the oven to 425°F (220°C). Line a small baking sheet with baking parchment.

Place the salmon on the lined baking sheet, drizzle with the olive oil, and season generously with salt. Top each filet with a few slices of lemon, sliced jalapeño, and garlic. Bake in the oven for 10 minutes, or until the salmon is cooked and flakes easily with a fork.

Meanwhile, for the crispy capers, pour the oil into a small, heavy skillet over medium heat and add the capers. Fry for a few minutes moving them around with a slotted spoon until the capers have turned golden, popped, and gone crispy. Remove with a slotted spoon onto paper towels and set aside. Keep the remaining oil in the pan for later.

For the aioli, blend the mayonnaise, herbs, garlic, and lemon juice in a blender until smooth.

Place the skillet back over medium heat and add the spinach and lemon juice. Sauté for 2 minutes, or until the spinach is wilted. Season to taste with salt.

When the salmon is ready, remove it from the oven. To plate, dollop half of the aioli in the middle of each plate, top with the salmon, sprinkle over the capers, and serve with the wilted spinach and an extra lemon wedge.

15-MINUTE MEALS

15-MINUTE MEALS

Sesame sticky noodles

Serves: 2
Prep Time: 10 minutes
Cook Time: 5 minutes

These noodles are packed full of flavor, and can be made in 15 minutes. Serve warm or cold, so they are perfect if you want to take them on a picnic. If you don't like too much spice, then add less chili oil.

14 ounces (400 g) dried ramen noodles
1 tablespoon toasted sesame oil
2 tablespoons soy sauce
1 tablespoon rice vinegar
1 tablespoon maple syrup
3 tablespoons tahini
1 tablespoon crunchy chili oil (I used Laoganma)
1 tablespoon miso paste
1 garlic clove, finely grated
1-inch (2.5 cm) piece of ginger, peeled and grated
2 tablespoons hot water
2 scallions, green part finely sliced
1 small carrot, julienned
½ cucumber, julienned
1 handful of toasted peanuts, chopped
1 tablespoon toasted sesame seeds
Cilantro leaves, for garnishing
½ lime, cut into wedges, for serving

Bring a medium pot of water to a boil, then cook the noodles according to the package directions, or until just tender. Drain and rinse under cold water to stop them cooking and set aside.

Whisk the sesame oil, soy sauce, rice vinegar, maple syrup, tahini, chili oil, and miso together in a medium bowl until smooth. Stir in the grated garlic and ginger, then pour in the hot water and mix until glossy.

Add the cooked noodles to the sauce bowl and mix well until coated. Add the scallions, carrot, and cucumber, then divide between two bowls. Top with the peanuts, sesame seeds, and cilantro. Serve with lime wedges.

Red curry and coconut mussels

Serves: 2
Prep Time: 5 minutes
Cook Time: 10 minutes

This recipe is quick to make if you don't want to spend too much time in the kitchen. Use a good-quality red curry paste and make sure the mussels are fresh and alive when you purchase them.

- 1 pound (450 g) live mussels
- 1 tablespoon coconut oil
- 3 garlic cloves, sliced
- 1 lemongrass stalk, outer leaves removed and thinly sliced
- 3 tablespoons red curry paste (use less if you don't like it too spicy)
- 1 (13.5-ounce / 400 ml) can full-fat coconut milk
- 1 tablespoon fish sauce
- 1 teaspoon brown sugar
- Juice of 1 lime
- 2 large handfuls of Thai basil leaves
- 1 red chile, sliced
- Crusty bread or rice, for serving (optional)

Clean the mussels under cold running water. Remove the beards and discard any mussels that are open.

Melt the coconut oil in a large pot over medium heat. Add the garlic and lemongrass and fry for 2 minutes. Add the curry paste and fry for 1 minute.

Pour in the coconut milk and fill the can halfway with water. Add this to the pot with the fish sauce and sugar, and bring to a simmer.

Add the mussels, increase the heat to high, and cover with a lid. Cook for 5 to 7 minutes, giving the pan a good shake occasionally until the mussels have opened.

Remove from the heat and discard any mussels that haven't opened. Squeeze in the lime juice, stir in the Thai basil, and sprinkle over the chile. Ladle the mussels and broth into two bowls. Serve with crusty bread or rice, if desired.

15-MINUTE MEALS 17

Spicy tuna tostadas with jalapeño avocado guacamole

Serves: 2
Prep time: 10 minutes
Cook time: 10 minutes

These tostadas are crunchy, zingy, and fresh, and the ideal dinner with a cold beer or a spicy margarita (see page 174) for a hot summer's evening. Make sure to source sushi-grade tuna.

¾ cup (180 ml) peanut oil
9 ounces (255 g) sushi-grade tuna, diced into ½-inch (1 cm) chunks
1 tablespoon soy sauce
1 teaspoon sesame oil
1 teaspoon rice wine vinegar
1 teaspoon sriracha
2 scallions, green parts only finely chopped
3 tablespoons chopped cilantro
6 small corn tortillas
1 ripe avocado
Juice of 1 lime
1 small jalapeño chile, finely chopped
¼ cucumber, finely diced
1 tablespoon toasted white and black sesame seeds
1 tablespoon kewpie mayonnaise
Salt

Heat the peanut oil in a medium skillet over medium heat.

Meanwhile, mix the diced tuna, soy sauce, sesame oil, rice vinegar, sriracha, scallions, and 1 tablespoon of the cilantro together in a medium bowl until combined. Chill in the refrigerator.

Line a baking sheet with paper towels. Test whether the oil is hot in the skillet by placing a corner of a tortilla in it. If it sizzles and starts to color, it's ready.

Fry a couple of tortillas at a time for 1 minute on each side, then carefully remove them with tongs and let drain on the lined baking sheet. Continue until all the tortillas are fried.

Meanwhile, scoop out the flesh of the avocado into a bowl and discard the pit. Squeeze the lime juice over the avocado, and stir in the jalapeño. Mash well with a fork and season to taste with salt. Stir in the remaining chopped cilantro.

When ready to serve, I like to build mine at the table. Spoon the guacamole over the tortilla, top with the tuna, some diced cucumber, a sprinkle of sesame seeds, and a squeeze of mayonnaise. Serve immediately.

15-MINUTE MEALS 19

Shortcut miso ramen

Serves: 2
Prep Time: 5 minutes
Cook Time: 10 minutes

This dish is packed full of flavor and goodness, and perfect for a midweek meal. You can add anything you normally love to your ramen, top it with roasted leftover pork, barbecued chicken, or even some quick pan-fried shrimp.

2 medium eggs
1 tablespoon sesame oil
1½-inch (4 cm) piece of ginger, peeled and julienned
5 garlic cloves, sliced
3⅓ cups (800 ml) good-quality chicken stock
2 tablespoons miso paste
1 tablespoon light soy sauce
2 packages instant ramen noodles
1 carrot, julienned
1 head bok choy, finely sliced
4 snack nori sheets
1 tablespoon chili oil
1 tablespoon pickled red onions

Place a small saucepan over medium heat and fill with water. Bring to a boil, then add the eggs and reduce to a simmer. Boil the eggs for 7 minutes. Drain and plunge into ice-cold water.

Meanwhile, add the sesame oil to a medium pot and place over medium heat. Add the ginger and garlic and fry for 2 minutes. Pour in the stock and bring to a simmer.

Add the miso and soy sauce to the stock and whisk well until all the miso has blended in. Add the instant noodles to the broth, discarding the sachets they come with, and boil for 4 minutes.

Remove from the heat and add the carrot and bok choy.

Peel the cooked eggs and slice them in half. Ladle the noodles and vegetables into two bowls. Pour over the broth and top with the egg and nori. Drizzle over the chili oil and finish with the red onions. Eat immediately.

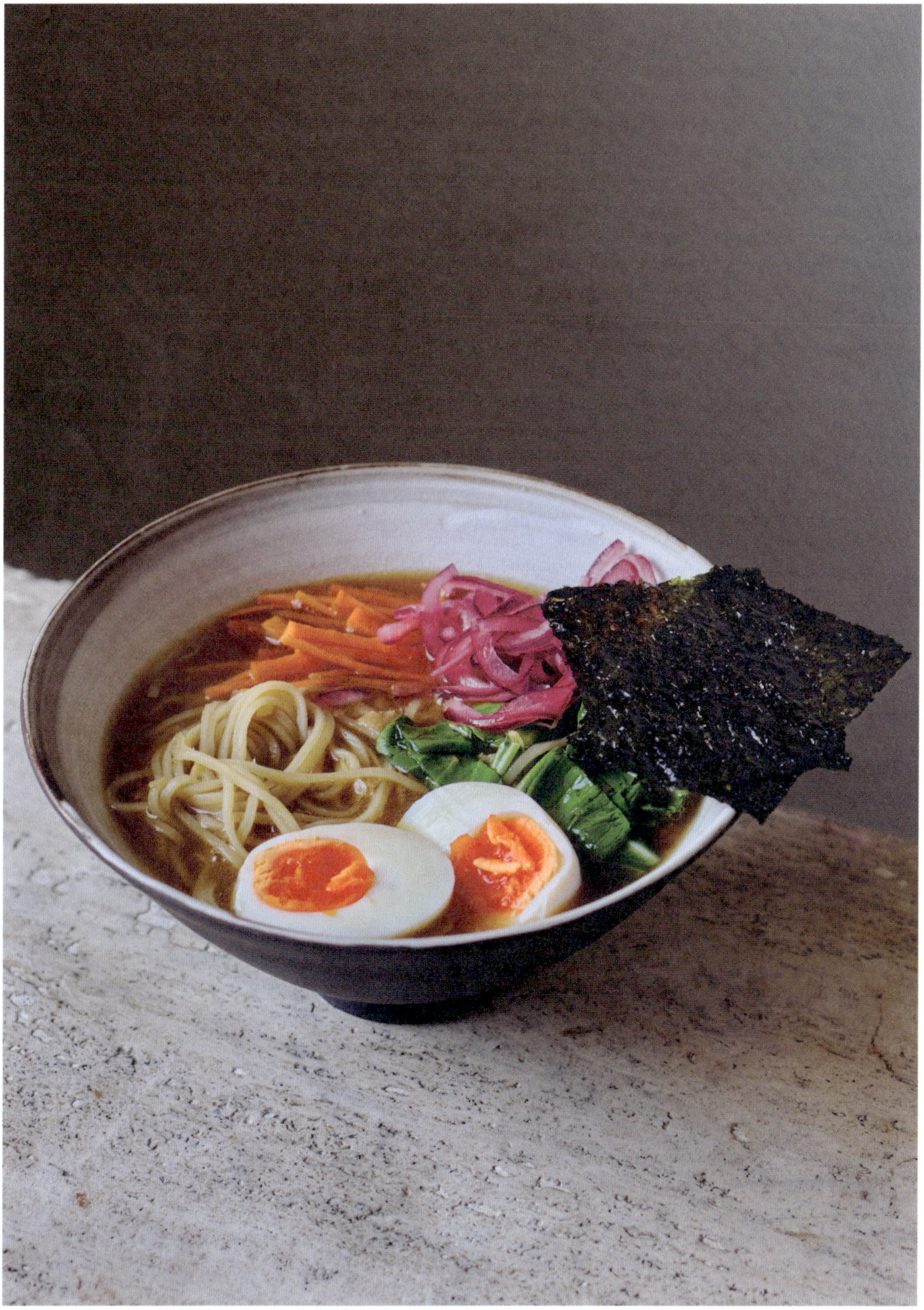

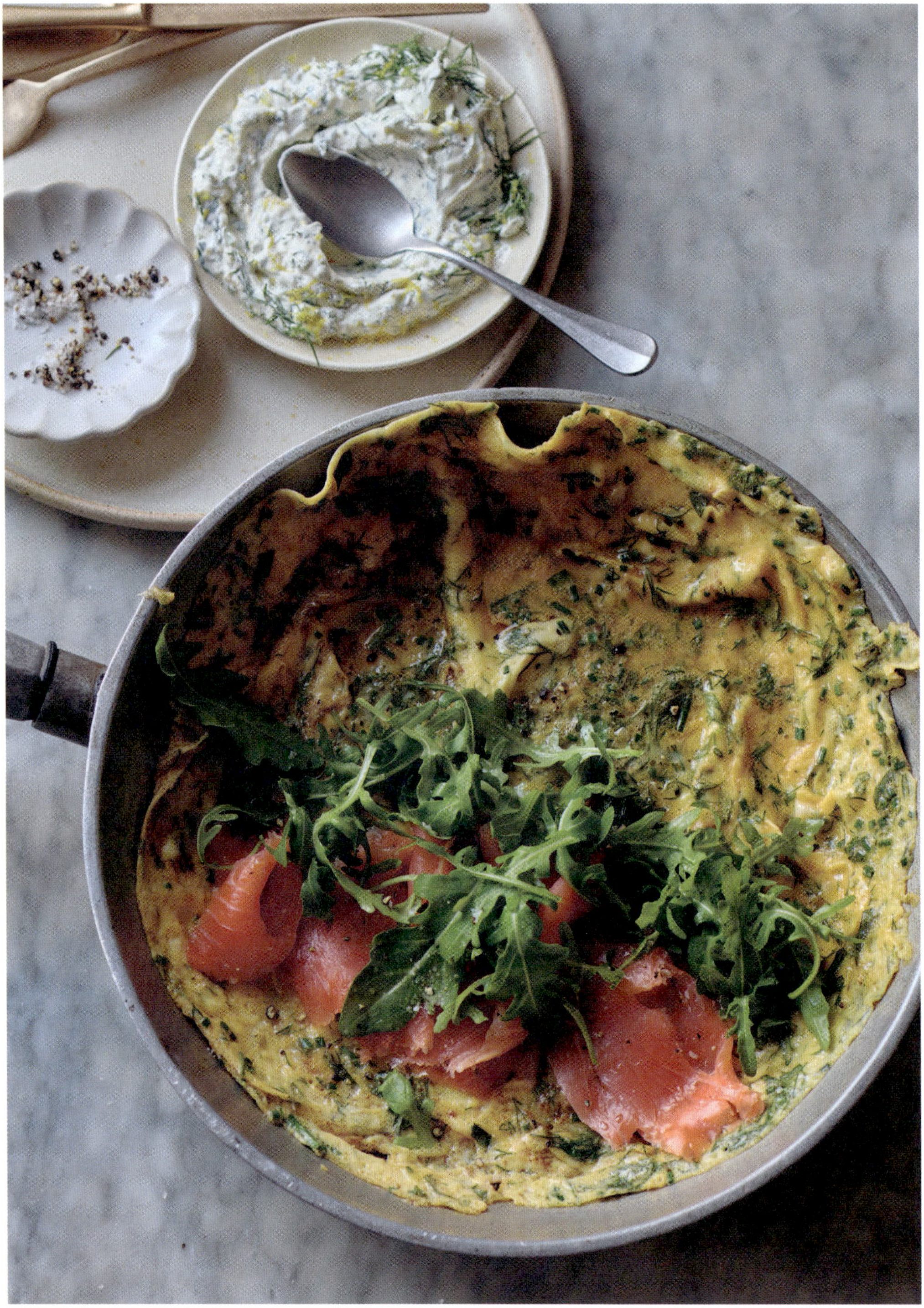

The perfect smoked salmon omelet with chive and dill crème fraîche

This omelet can be put together in under 20 minutes. I make one large omelet, which saves on cleaning-up. Feel free to add whatever your favorite combination is—cheese and ham always wins.

Serves: 2
Prep Time: 10 minutes
Cook Time: 10 minutes

5 medium eggs
2 tablespoons heavy cream
2 tablespoons chopped chives
2 tablespoons chopped dill
1 tablespoon chopped tarragon
Scant ½ cup (100 g) crème fraîche
½ unwaxed lemon
2 tablespoons salted butter
3½ ounces (100 g) smoked salmon
1 large handful of arugula
Salt and freshly ground black pepper

In a medium bowl, mix the eggs and cream together well. Mix in half the chives, dill, and tarragon, and season with salt and pepper.

In another bowl, mix the crème fraîche with the remaining herbs and grate in the lemon zest. Season to taste and set aside.

Place a large nonstick skillet over medium heat. Add the butter and watch until it begins to foam but not brown. Pour in the egg mixture.

Using a spatula, pull the omelet away from the edge of the pan into the middle, angling the pan so the egg runs back into the bit you have just exposed. Do this another four or five times in different places, so you have undulating waves of the egg. Let cook until the omelet is almost set, 1 to 2 minutes.

Remove from the heat, lay the salmon over the top of the omelet, then sprinkle over the arugula. Flip the omelet out of the pan. Slice in half and serve immediately.

24   15-MINUTE MEALS

Fried lemon spaghetti

Serves: 2
Prep Time: 3 minutes
Cook Time: 12 minutes

Frying the lemon in this recipe makes the most umami, citrus, and savory pasta. It is perfect for the nights when you have little in the pantry but want something delicious, too. It's fresh and hearty.

2 slices of sourdough bread
½ cup (110 g) salted butter
9 ounces (255 g) dried spaghetti
Scant ½ cup (100 ml) good-quality olive oil
1 lemon, chopped and seeded
4 garlic cloves, sliced
1 teaspoon fennel seeds
1 teaspoon red pepper flakes
Juice of 1 lemon
⅓ cup (35 g) grated Parmesan, plus extra for serving
1 handful of basil leaves
Salt and freshly ground black pepper

Place a large saucepan filled with water over high heat and season generously with salt.

Chop or blitz the sourdough bread into tiny pieces, slightly coarser than breadcrumbs. Place a large skillet over medium heat and add 1 tablespoon of the butter. Add the bread and toast, moving the bread around until golden and crisp, 3 minutes. Season with salt, tip onto a plate, and set aside.

Once the water is boiling, add the pasta, and cook until it is al dente, about 7 minutes. Drain, setting a ladleful of the pasta water aside.

Meanwhile, add the olive oil, chopped lemon, and garlic to the skillet and fry for 2 minutes over medium heat until the lemon starts to catch and turn golden. Add the fennel seeds and red pepper flakes and reduce the heat to low. Add the cooked pasta to the pan, tossing it very well.

Add the reserved pasta cooking water, most of the Parmesan, and the remaining butter to the pan and toss constantly until the pasta is glossy. Add the lemon juice and season well with salt and pepper.

Divide between two plates and top with the breadcrumbs, a little extra cheese, and the basil.

Thai basil and chicken stir-fry with a crispy egg

Serves: 2
Prep Time: 5 minutes
Cook Time: 8 minutes

I love Thailand so much. The food is out of this world, and this is one of my go-to midweek meals. It's packed full of all the things I want. It's spicy but not fiery, so trust me with the chile amount. Try to find Thai basil for the best flavor.

- 4 garlic cloves, peeled but left whole
- 3 red Thai chiles
- 2 teaspoons light soy sauce
- 2 teaspoons dark soy sauce
- 2 tablespoons oyster sauce
- 1 teaspoon palm sugar or brown sugar
- 2 tablespoons water
- 2 tablespoons peanut oil
- 2 boneless chicken breasts, about 7 ounces (200 g), cut into 1-inch (2.5 cm) chunks
- 4 scallions, green parts thinly sliced and white parts cut into 1-inch (2.5 cm) pieces
- 2 medium eggs
- 1 large handful of Thai basil leaves
- Steamed rice, for serving

This comes together quickly, so start with the prep. Add the peeled garlic and chiles to a mortar and pestle, and bash until the chiles and garlic turn mushy.

Place a wok or large skillet over high heat.

Mix the soy sauces, oyster sauce, sugar, and water together in a small bowl. Set aside.

Once the wok is hot, add 1 tablespoon of the oil to the wok. Add the garlic and chile mix and fry, stirring quickly, for 1 minute until fragrant. Add the chicken and fry, tossing frequently for 2 minutes. Add the white parts of the scallions and fry for another minute. Add the sauce and reduce the heat to medium.

Place a small skillet over high heat and add the remaining tablespoon of oil. Once the oil is very hot, add the eggs, and fry until golden on the edges and starting to go crisp, but the yolks are still runny, about 2 minutes.

Stir the basil into the chicken and remove from the heat. Divide between plates, then top with the fried eggs and sprinkle over the remaining sliced scallions. Serve with rice.

15-MINUTE MEALS

Crispy gnocchi with corn, ricotta, and spinach

Creamy corn and crispy gnocchi make such an excellent midweek meal. To make this vegetarian, use vegetable stock instead of the chicken stock.

Serves: 2
Prep Time: 3 minutes
Cook Time: 12 minutes

2 ears of corn
1 tablespoon salted butter
2 garlic cloves, thinly sliced
1 red chile, thinly sliced
2 scallions, thinly sliced with white and green parts separated
Scant ½ cup (100 ml) chicken stock
Scant ½ cup (100 g) ricotta
1 teaspoon miso paste
1 tablespoon olive oil
10 ounces (280 g) gnocchi
2 cups (100 g) baby leaf spinach
Salt

Place a large saucepan filled with water over medium heat and season well with salt. Bring to a boil, then add the corn and cook for 2 minutes. Remove with tongs and set aside. Set the pan with the water aside.

Add the butter to a large skillet and place over medium heat. Slice the kernels off the corn and add them to the pan along with the garlic and chile. Add the white parts of the scallions and fry until the corn starts to go golden.

Tip the corn mix into a food processor, add the chicken stock, ricotta, and miso, and blend until smooth. Wipe the pan and place it over medium heat with the olive oil.

Bring the reserved corn water to a boil, then add the gnocchi and cook until they float to the surface, about 1 minute. Scoop out with a slotted spoon and carefully tip into the skillet. Fry the gnocchi on each side until golden and crisp, 4 minutes in total. Reduce the heat and add the spinach. Wilt until all the water has evaporated. Add the corn sauce and mix well. Toss the remaining scallions over the top and serve.

15-MINUTE MEALS

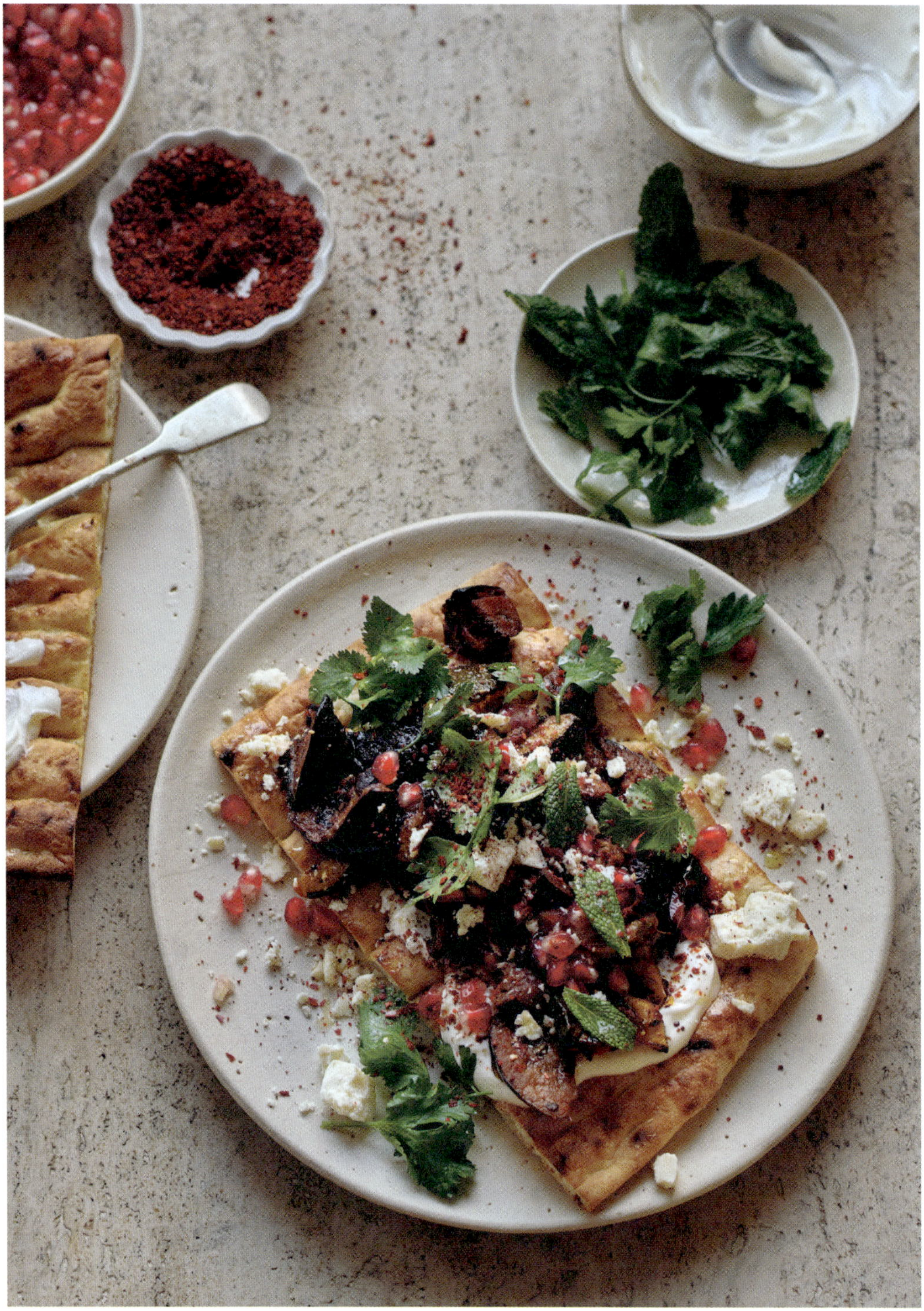

Harissa charred vegetables with flatbread, and spiked yogurt

Serves: 2
Prep Time: 2 minutes
Cook Time: 15 minutes

You can double or triple this recipe, then store the vegetables in the refrigerator and either eat them on their own or serve them with crispy chicken thighs or even lamb koftas for a special meal for someone. I cook the vegetables under a very hot broiler as this caramelizes them quickly, but if you have more time, you can roast them in an oven preheated to 400°F (200°C) for 40 minutes.

1 zucchini, cut into ¾-inch (2 cm) chunks
1 eggplant, cut into ¾-inch (2 cm) chunks
1 red bell pepper, cut into ¾-inch (2 cm) chunks
7 ounces (200 g) cherry tomatoes, halved
3 tablespoons harissa paste
Juice of 1 lemon, divided
1 tablespoon olive oil
1 red onion, quartered
6 garlic cloves, smashed
1 teaspoon cumin seeds
1 teaspoon coriander seeds
⅔ cup (160 g) whole Greek yogurt
1 teaspoon chile flakes, such as Aleppo
2 flatbreads
1 handful of pomegranate seeds
1 handful of mint, cilantro, and parsley leaves
⅓ cup (50 g) crumbled feta
Salt

Preheat the broiler to maximum.

Arrange the zucchini, eggplant, and red bell pepper on a large baking sheet. Add the cherry tomatoes, 2 tablespoons of the harissa, half of the lemon juice, and the olive oil. Using your hands, mix very well.

Mix in the onion and garlic, and stir through the cumin and coriander seeds. Season with salt and mix well. Broil for 4 minutes.

Meanwhile, in a bowl, mix the remaining tablespoon of harissa with the yogurt and remaining lemon juice. Season with salt and a sprinkle of the chile flakes.

Stir the vegetables to mix, then broil for another 9 minutes, stirring occasionally, or until they start to catch and turn golden.

Remove the vegetables and set aside, then broil the breads until toasted, about 1 minute.

Spread the breads with the yogurt mix, top with the broiled vegetables, and sprinkle over the pomegranate seeds, herbs, and feta. Serve with extra chile flakes.

Creamy cashew green pasta

Serves: 2
Prep Time: 7 minutes
Cook Time: 8 minutes

If you would like to make this pasta dish vegan, then just omit the burrata at the end. The earthy Tuscan kale in this recipe works so well, but if it's not in season, then use spinach instead.

1¼ cups (150 g) cashews
2 garlic cloves, peeled but left whole
Zest and juice of 1 lemon
2 tablespoons nutritional yeast
1 bunch of basil
Scant ½ cup (100 ml) extra-virgin olive oil, plus extra for drizzling
7 ounces (200 g) kale, such as Tuscan kale, leaves shredded
9 ounces (255 g) paccheri pasta or rigatoni
1 large pinch of red pepper flakes
1 (6 ounces / 170 g) ball of burrata
⅓ cup (50 g) chopped roasted smoked almonds
Salt

Place a large saucepan filled with water over medium heat and season well with salt.

Add the cashews to a medium heatproof bowl and pour over enough boiling water to cover.

Blend the garlic, lemon zest and juice, nutritional yeast, majority of the basil, and olive oil in a blender until mostly smooth.

Drain the cashews and add to the blender.

Once the water has come to a boil, add the kale and blanch for 1 minute. Remove with tongs into a colander; add the pasta to the pan, and cook until it is al dente, about 7 minutes.

Add the kale to the blender and blitz until smooth. Season to taste, then blitz in the red pepper flakes.

Scoop the green sauce into a heatproof bowl. Once the pasta is cooked, drain, reserving a ladleful of the pasta water, and add the pasta to the sauce and mix well. Add the pasta cooking water and mix again. Tip onto a serving platter and top with the burrata. Finish with the chopped almonds, remaining basil, and a good drizzle of olive oil.

15-MINUTE MEALS   33

Salmon tikka skewers with a cilantro marinade

Serves: 2
Prep Time: 5 minutes
Cook Time: 10 minutes

An amazing friend and brilliant Indian cook, Maunika, once made me her delicious tikka-style salmon. Here, I make it into skewers and simplify the ingredients a little. Serve with rotis or parathas and mango chutney.

3 garlic cloves, peeled but left whole
1½-inch (4 cm) piece of ginger, peeled
Juice of 1 lime, divided
1 tablespoon vegetable oil
¾ pound (350 g) skinless salmon filets, cut into 2-inch (5 cm) chunks
1 cup (20 g) coarsely chopped basil
1 cup (40 g) coarsely chopped cilantro
2 green Thai chiles
⅛ teaspoon garam masala
2 tablespoons Greek yogurt
½ cucumber, chopped
8 cherry tomatoes, chopped
2 roti
1 tablespoon pickled red onions
Salt

Preheat the broiler to medium to high.

In a small blender, blend 2 garlic cloves and the ginger to a rough paste.

Add the paste to a large bowl along with half the lime juice, oil, and salmon. Mix well.

In the same blender, add the basil, ¾ cup (30 g) of the cilantro, the chiles, the remaining garlic clove, the garam masala, yogurt, and a good pinch of salt and blend until smooth.

Add the paste to the salmon in the bowl and mix well. Thread the salmon onto four metal or bamboo skewers, then broil, basting with any of the remaining marinade, until the salmon is just cooked through, 6 to 8 minutes.

Meanwhile, in a medium bowl, toss the chopped cucumber, tomatoes, and remaining cilantro together with some salt and the rest of the lime juice. Set aside.

Once the salmon is cooked, remove from the broiler and toast the rotis either in a dry skillet or under the broiler until warmed through.

Place the skewers on the rotis, top with the cucumber-tomato mix and pickled onions, and serve immediately.

15-MINUTE MEALS

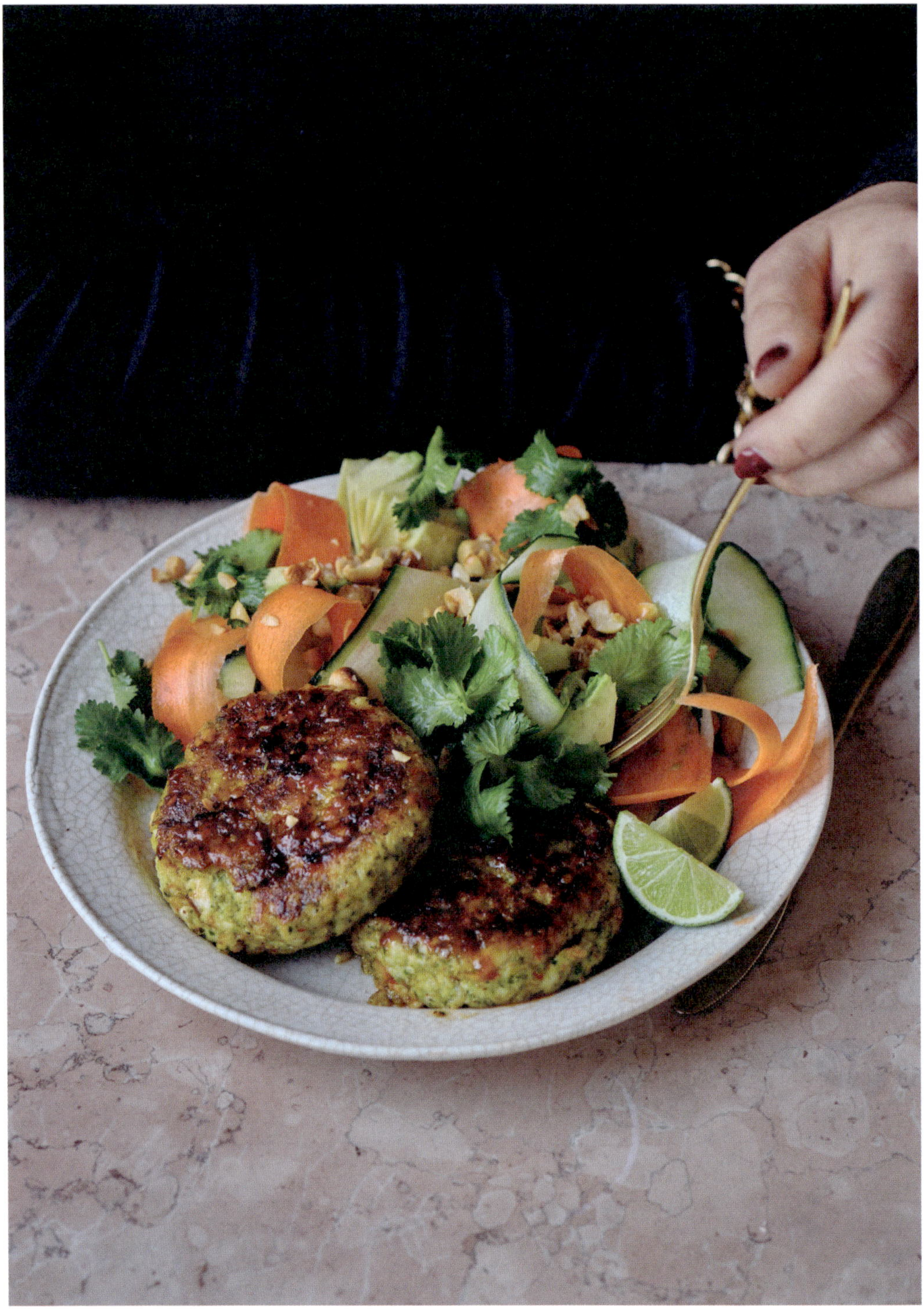

Lemongrass fish cakes with avocado and carrot salad

Serves: 2
Prep Time: 10 minutes
Cook Time: 5 minutes

These fragrant fish cakes are a brilliant midweek meal for someone special. You can make the cakes ahead of time and chill them for up to 24 hours in the refrigerator. The sticky sweet chili sauce at the end is something I enjoyed while traveling in Asia, and it was such a game-changer.

2 lemongrass stalks, cut in half lengthwise, outer skin removed, and coarsely chopped
3 cups (60 g) bunch of cilantro, divided
4 scallions, coarsely chopped
1½-inch (4 cm) piece of ginger, peeled and sliced
2 garlic cloves, peeled but left whole
2 red chiles
14 ounces (400 g) skinless boneless cod filets, coarsely chopped
¼ cup (60 g) rice flour
1 tablespoon peanut oil
1 carrot
½ cucumber
1 tablespoon crushed toasted peanuts
Zest and juice of 1 lime
1 avocado, peeled, pitted, and flesh chopped
2 tablespoons sweet chili sauce
Salt

Pulse the lemongrass, half the cilantro, the scallions, ginger, garlic, and chiles in a food processor until it is a smoothish paste.

Add the cod and rice flour and pulse until it just forms a dough but isn't smooth. Using clean hands, shape the fishcakes into four equal patties.

Heat the oil in a large skillet over medium heat. Fry the cakes for 2 to 3 minutes on each side until they feel springy when gently prodded with a finger.

Meanwhile, using a vegetable peeler, peel long strips of the carrot and cucumber into a bowl. Tear in the remaining cilantro and toss through the peanuts. Squeeze over half of the lime juice and add all the zest, then season with salt. Add the avocado and toss it all together.

Once the fishcakes have cooked through, add the sweet chili sauce to the skillet and fry, moving the pan around, until the fishcakes are coated and a little sticky.

Using a spatula, carefully scoop the fishcakes onto two plates and serve with the salad and a lime wedge on the side.

Farinata-style pancakes, jarred vegetable salad, and lemon zest ricotta

Serves: 2
Prep Time: 5 minutes
Cook Time: 10 minutes

In Italy, they make the most delicious trays of gram (chickpea) flour farinata. It is baked in oil and takes some time, so this is my speedy version for you. The pancakes will last about four days in the refrigerator, so you can double up the recipe and then top them with whatever is in your pantry for another meal.

2 cups (250 g) gram (chickpea) flour
1½ cups (360 ml) oat milk
1 teaspoon fennel seeds
1 small bunch of thyme, leaves picked
Olive oil, for frying
Zest and juice of 1 lemon
1 red chile, diced
Scant ½ cup (100 g) ricotta
5-ounce (140 g) jar mixed charred vegetables in olive oil, or a mix of artichokes, bell peppers, and zucchini charred in oil
Salt
1 handful of dill leaves, for garnish

Add the flour to a large bowl, then pour over the oat milk. Whisk until smooth, then add the fennel seeds, thyme, and a good pinch of salt.

Place a large skillet over medium to high heat and add enough oil to cover the bottom of the pan in a thin layer. Pour in a ladleful of the batter, or enough to cover the bottom, and fry until set and crisp on one side, 2 minutes. Flip over and fry for another 30 seconds. Remove from the pan and fry the remaining pancakes in the same way.

When the pancakes are cooked, add the lemon zest and chile to a small bowl. Add the ricotta and whisk until smooth. Drain the vegetables from the oil.

Top the pancakes with a scoop of ricotta and the vegetables. Garnish with dill and serve with a squeeze of lemon juice before eating.

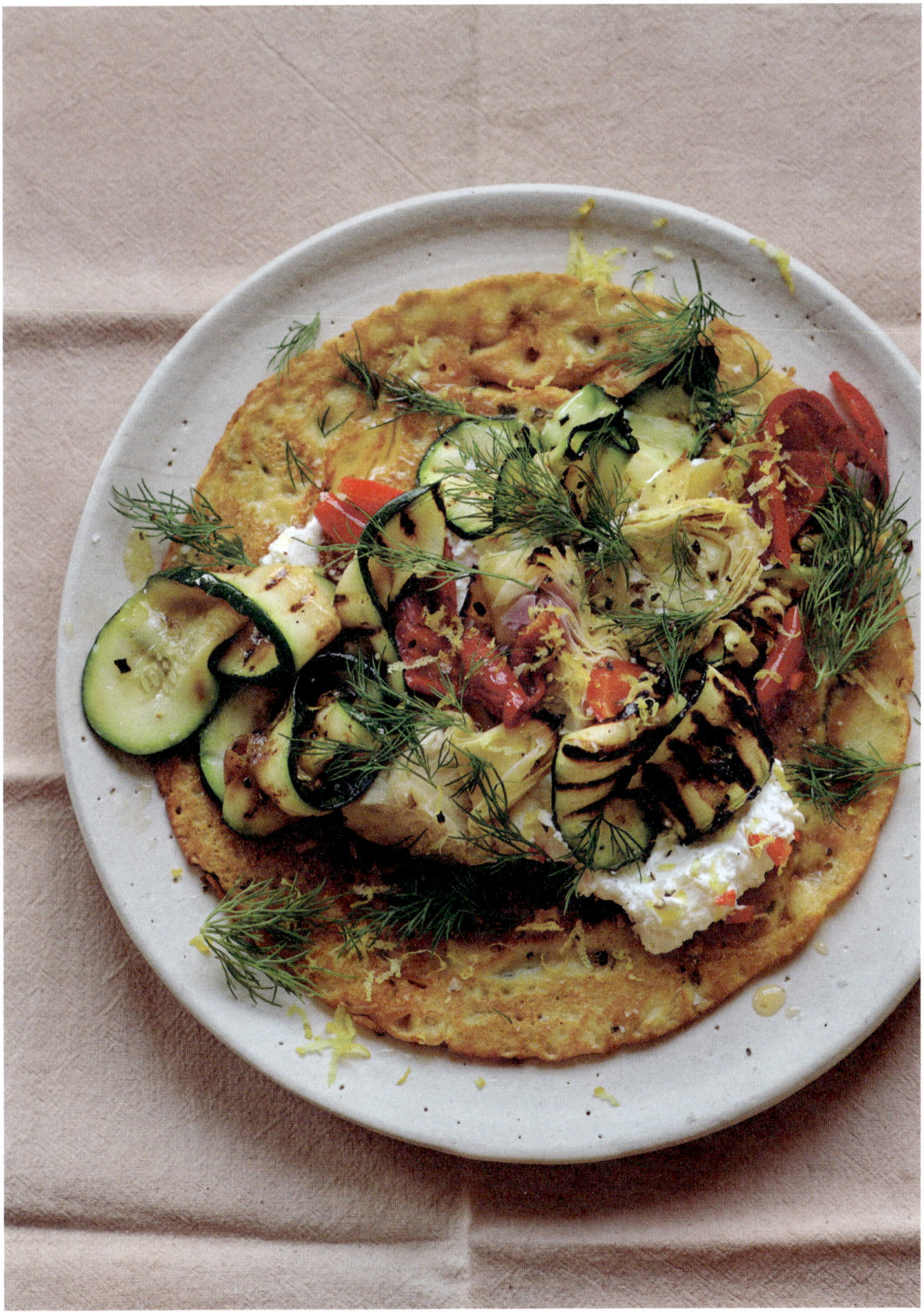

15-MINUTE MEALS

Lebanese chopped salad

Serves: 2
Prep Time: 7 minutes
Cook Time: 10 minutes

This salad is packed full of flavor and so satisfying. If you don't eat halloumi, baked feta works well and if you are dairy-free, 1 cup (140 g) of chickpeas is great tossed in too.

1 pita
1 tablespoon olive oil
1 tablespoon za'atar
1 (8-ounce / 225 g) halloumi, cut into ¾-inch (2 cm) chunks
1 tablespoon honey
7 ounces (200 g) cherry tomatoes, cut into 1¼-inch (3 cm) chunks
½ cucumber, cut into 1¼-inch (3 cm) chunks
½ red onion, cut into 1¼-inch (3 cm) slices
1 head of romaine lettuce
1 cup (30 g) chopped mint
1 cup (30 g) chopped parsley

FOR THE DRESSING
1 garlic clove, grated
1 teaspoon sumac, plus extra for sprinkling
Juice of 1 lemon
2 tablespoons olive oil
1 tablespoon pomegranate molasses
Salt

Preheat the oven to 400°F (200°C).

Tear the pita into bite-size pieces and arrange them on a large baking sheet. Drizzle over the olive oil and sprinkle with the za'atar. Using your hands, mix very well, making sure the pita are really well coated.

Put the pita onto a third of the baking sheet and add the halloumi to the remaining space. Drizzle over the honey and bake for 10 minutes, tossing the halloumi halfway through, until the pita is crisp and golden.

Meanwhile, toss the tomatoes, cucumber, and onion together in a large bowl. Cut the lettuce into roughly the same size bits as the vegetables and add to the bowl with the chopped mint and parsley. Set aside.

For the dressing, add the garlic, sumac, lemon juice, olive oil, and pomegranate molasses to a small clean jar, seal the jar and shake to emulsify. Season well with salt and shake again.

Toss the pita and halloumi into the salad and pour over the dressing. Sprinkle over a little extra sumac and serve immediately.

FRIENDSH

FEEDING

TIPS

My perfect Caesar

Serves: 2
Prep Time: 5 minutes
Cook Time: 35 minutes

As a chef and food writer, I often get asked what my last meal would consist of. It would be a few small plates, but one of them would be this salad. The croutons are next-level delicious. As the chicken cooks, it releases its fats into the bread, making it unbelievable. You'll never make a Caesar any other way again, and you're welcome!

5 chicken thighs, skin-on and bone-in
1 (7-ounce / 200 g) half-baked ciabatta, torn into bite-size chunks
1 tablespoon olive oil
1 garlic head, halved
3 rosemary stalks
2 tablespoons capers, drained
½ lemon
3½ ounces (100 g) green beans
1 head of romaine lettuce
Grated Parmesan, for sprinkling
Salt

FOR THE DRESSING

6 anchovy filets from a tin in olive oil
½ cup (50 g) grated Parmesan
Scant ½ cup (100 g) plain yogurt
1½ teaspoons Dijon mustard
Juice of ½ lemon

Preheat the oven to 375°F (190°C).

Season the chicken thighs generously with salt, then place them skin-side down in a nonstick skillet. Place the skillet over medium heat and fry until the skin is very crispy, 8 minutes.

Spread the ciabatta pieces out in an 8 by 12-inch (20 by 30 cm) baking dish. Drizzle over the olive oil, then add the garlic, rosemary, capers, and squeeze over the lemon juice. Add the lemon half and mix well.

Arrange the chicken thighs on top of the bread and pour over any juices from the skillet. Roast the chicken for 20 minutes, or until the thighs are cooked through.

Meanwhile, place the skillet over high heat, add the green beans, and fry until charred, 6 minutes. Season with salt and fry for 1 minute. Remove from the heat and let cool.

Once the chicken thighs are done, place them on a plate. Mix the bread in the dish and return it to the oven until crisp, 15 to 20 minutes.

For the dressing, blend the anchovies, Parmesan, yogurt, mustard, and lemon juice in a small blender until smooth. Remove half the garlic from the bread dish and add it to the blender, blitzing again. If your dressing is too thick, add a little water to loosen.

Slice the chicken into strips and set aside. Discard the bones.

Pour half the dressing onto a platter and tear over the lettuce, using two forks to give it a good mix until all the leaves are dressed. Add the green beans and top with the chicken. Sprinkle the croutons and the bits from the dish over the top, then drizzle with the remaining dressing. Sprinkle with Parmesan and serve.

Steak and chimichurri with garlic potatoes

Serves: 2
Prep Time: 5 minutes
Cook Time: 45 minutes

Sharing a large steak with spiced chimichurri and crunchy roast potatoes feels decadent, yet is very easy to whip up. I like to open a good bottle of red wine and eat this with my best friend—it is a perfect evening for me.

1 pound (450 g) new baby potatoes
1 tablespoon olive oil, plus extra for drizzling
1 (1½-pounds / 680 g) bone-in rib eye steak, at room temperature an hour before cooking
Salt

FOR THE GARLIC BUTTER

2 tablespoons salted butter, at room temperature
3 garlic cloves, grated
⅔ cup (60 g) grated Parmesan, divided

FOR THE CHIMICHURRI

1 cup (30 g) chopped parsley
1 tablespoon dried oregano
1 garlic clove, grated
1 tablespoon red wine vinegar
1 teaspoon red pepper flakes, or to taste
6 tablespoons olive oil
Juice of ½ lemon
½ teaspoon salt

Preheat the oven to 400°F (200°C).

Bring a medium saucepan of water to a boil. Add the potatoes and cook until they are soft in the middle, 10 to 15 minutes. Drain and set aside.

Meanwhile, for the garlic butter, mix the butter, garlic, and 3 tablespoons of the Parmesan together in a bowl until well combined.

Tip the potatoes onto a large baking sheet, and using the bottom of a mug or glass, press down until they squash into disks. Top with a spoonful of the garlic butter and drizzle over the oil. Season with salt and roast until deeply golden and crisp, 30 minutes.

For the chimichurri, mix the herbs, garlic, vinegar, red pepper flakes, oil, lemon juice, and salt together in a bowl. Taste and adjust the seasoning, if needed.

When the potatoes have 20 minutes left, place a heavy skillet over high heat. Season the steak on both sides with salt and drizzle with oil. When the pan is searing hot, add the steak and fry for 3 minutes, or until there is a deep brown crust. Turn over and cook for 3 minutes, then turn over again and cook for another 6 minutes, or until done to your liking. Remove the steak and let rest for 10 minutes. Cook for another 10 minutes in the oven if you like your steak well done.

Remove the potatoes from the oven and sprinkle over the remaining Parmesan. Scoop onto a platter, slice the steak, and lay next to the potatoes. Serve with the chimichurri.

FEEDING FRIENDSHIPS

Schnitzel and kohlrabi slaw

Schnitzel originates in Austria and is typically made with veal, but I love pork or even chicken here too. The cool, tart kohlrabi slaw adds a nice balance to round out the plate.

Serves: 2
Prep Time: 20 minutes
Cook Time: 6 minutes

2 (7 ounces / 200 g) boneless pork loin chops
¾ cup (100 g) all-purpose flour
1 teaspoon crushed fennel seeds
2 eggs
3½ cups (150 g) panko breadcrumbs
Scant ½ cup (100 ml) peanut or vegetable oil
6 sage leaves
1 handful of watercress
1 small handful of parsley leaves
Salt and pepper
Lemon wedges, for serving

FOR THE KOHLRABI SLAW
1 small kohlrabi
1 apple, preferably Pink Lady
Scant ½ cup (100 g) crème fraîche
1 tablespoon wholegrain mustard
Zest and juice of ½ lemon
Salt and pepper

For the slaw, peel the kohlrabi, then slice it into matchsticks, and add it to a large bowl.

Core the apple and slice into similar-size matchsticks as the kohlrabi. Add to the bowl with the crème fraîche, mustard, and lemon zest and juice, and mix. Season well with salt and pepper and chill in the refrigerator until needed.

Place one pork chop on a large piece of baking parchment and fold over the parchment to cover, making sure it's large enough to cover three times. Using a meat mallet or a rolling pin, evenly bash the meat until it is ¾-inch (2 cm) thick. You will need to keep moving it around to ensure it is evenly flattened. Do the same with the remaining chop.

Add the flour to a wide bowl, season with salt and pepper, and mix in the fennel seeds. Whisk the eggs in another wide bowl, then add the panko breadcrumbs to a third wide bowl and season with salt.

Heat the oil in your largest skillet over medium heat. Line a large plate with paper towels.

Meanwhile, dip one of the pork chops into the flour and toss until it is evenly coated on each side. Tap off any excess flour, then dip it into the egg, moving it around until it is fully coated. Place three sage leaves on one side of the chop, then toss in the breadcrumbs, making sure the pork is coated all over. Place it on a large plate and repeat with the remaining chop.

Place the schnitzels in the hot skillet and fry for 3 minutes on each side, or until golden and crisp all over. Remove them from the pan and let stand on the lined plate for a minute.

Serve the schnitzels with the slaw, watercress, parsley, and a lemon wedge.

Pasta alla norma with crispy capers and ricotta salata

This is my sister's favorite pasta dish, so when we get together, she always requests it. I couldn't write a book on cooking for two without including our special meal. I used paccheri pasta for this dish, but use any pasta you like.

Serves: 2
Prep Time: 15 minutes
Cook Time: 15 minutes

3 tablespoons capers, drained
⅓ cup (80 ml) extra-virgin olive oil, plus extra for drizzling
3 garlic cloves, thinly sliced
1 large eggplant, sliced into ¾-inch (2 cm) chunks
1 (14-ounce / 400 g) can good-quality plum tomatoes
1 large pinch of red pepper flakes
¼ teaspoon brown sugar
10 ounces (280 g) pasta of your choice
¾ cup (20 g) basil leaves
2 tablespoons ricotta salata, grated
Salt

Add the capers to a medium pot. Pour over the oil and set over medium heat. Fry the capers for 4 minutes, tossing frequently. Add the garlic and fry until the capers have popped and gone crisp and the garlic is golden. Using a slotted spoon, scoop them out into a bowl and set aside.

Add the chopped eggplant to the pot, season with salt, and fry, stirring frequently, until softened and golden, 10 minutes. Once all the eggplant is golden and soft, remove half from the pot and set aside.

Add the tomatoes to the pot, then add half of the reserved garlic and capers. Cook until the tomato sauce has reduced and become thick. Season with salt and red pepper flakes. Stir in the sugar and leave over low heat.

Meanwhile, bring a large saucepan of water to a boil. Season generously with salt, add the pasta, and cook according to the package directions, or until al dente.

Drain the pasta, reserving half a mugful of cooking water. Remove the sauce from the heat and add the pasta, stirring until the pasta is coated in the sauce, adding a little of the reserved pasta water, at a time until the sauce is velvety.

Add the reserved fried eggplant and capers-garlic mixture to the pasta. Top with the basil and grated ricotta, then add a drizzle of olive oil. Serve.

FEEDING FRIENDSHIPS 51

Niçoise salad with crispy green beans

I use a fresh tuna steak as I love the meaty seared filet in this salad, but if you can't purchase tuna steak then simply use good-quality jarred or canned tuna in olive oil. You can prepare the salad in advance and dress it at the last minute before serving.

Serves: 2
Prep Time: 10 minutes
Cook Time: 20 minutes

5 ounces (140 g) baby new potatoes, any large ones halved
2 eggs
7 ounces (200 g) green beans, trimmed
1 tablespoon olive oil, divided
1 teaspoon white mustard seeds
1 (½-pound / 225 g) tuna steak
2 small heads of gem lettuce, leaves torn
1 cup (100 g) black kalamata olives, pitted
3 ripe tomatoes, coarsely chopped
Salt and pepper

FOR THE DRESSING
Zest and juice of ½ unwaxed orange
1 small bunch of dill, leaves picked
1 tablespoon capers, drained
3 tablespoons olive oil
2 teaspoons wholegrain mustard
1 tablespoon red wine vinegar

Fill a medium pot with water and place over medium heat. Season with a good pinch of salt, and add the potatoes. Cook until soft when prodded with a fork, 15 minutes.

Meanwhile, have a bowl of ice-cold water nearby. Place a small saucepan of water over medium heat. Once simmering gently, add the eggs and boil for 8 minutes. Remove the eggs from the pan and place them into the bowl of ice-cold water. Set aside until needed.

Place a large skillet over high heat, Once the pan is very hot, add the green beans and fry until the beans catch and turn black in parts, 4 minutes. Drizzle over half the olive oil and remove from the heat. Sprinkle over the mustard seeds, then toast in the skillet for 1 minute. Tip the beans onto a platter and set aside.

Place the skillet back over high heat.

Meanwhile, for the dressing, blend the orange zest and juice, dill, capers, olive oil, mustard, and vinegar in a small blender until smooth. Set aside.

Once the potatoes are done, drain and spread them out onto the platter with the beans. Pour half the dressing over the potatoes and beans.

Drizzle the tuna with the remaining olive oil and season with salt and pepper. Place the tuna in the hot skillet and sear on each side for 2 minutes. Remove from the heat and rest.

Add the torn lettuce, olives, and chopped tomatoes to the platter. Peel the eggs, cut them into halves, and add to the platter. Slice the tuna, place it on top, and finish with a good sprinkle of salt and pepper and the remaining dressing.

Nasi lemak—coconut rice with sambal and a crispy egg

Serves: 2
Prep Time: 5 minutes
Cook Time: 20 minutes

I first ate this dish while traveling in Malaysia. It had almost sticky, fragrant coconut rice, which is served with a spicy sambal, toasted peanuts, and anchovies. Traditionally, dried anchovies are fried, but I love the oily tinned ones here. I eat mine with a crispy fried egg.

FOR THE COCONUT RICE
1⅓ cups (250 g) jasmine rice, washed well
Scant ½ cup (100 ml) full-fat coconut milk
¾ cup (180 ml) water
2 makrut lime leaves or 1 pandan leaf if you can get it
1 lemongrass stalk, outer leaves removed and bashed
1 teaspoon salt

FOR THE SAMBAL
1 ounce (30 g) dried long chiles
1 shallot, peeled
2 tablespoons macadamia nuts
3 Asian red chiles
1½-inch (4 cm) piece of ginger, peeled and grated
1 lemongrass stalk, the inner part only
2 teaspoons tamarind paste
1 teaspoon salt

FOR SERVING
2 tablespoons peanut oil
2 tablespoons raw peanuts
2 eggs
½ cucumber, sliced on the bias
1 (1.7-ounce / 47.5 g) tin anchovy filets in olive oil

For the sambal, place the dried chiles in a heatproof bowl and cover with boiling water. Set aside.

For the rice, add the rice to a medium pot with a tight-fitting lid. Pour in the coconut milk and water, then add the makrut or pandan leaves, and the lemongrass. Season with the salt and bring to a boil. Once boiling, stir, then cover with the lid. Reduce the heat to a low simmer and leave for 10 minutes. Turn off the heat and let stand for another 8 minutes untouched. Don't be tempted to peek!

Meanwhile, for the sambal, drain the dried chiles and add them to a food processor with the shallot, macadamia nuts, red chiles, ginger, and lemongrass, blending until you have a red paste.

Add the sambal paste to a small skillet and fry over medium to high heat, stirring frequently for 10 minutes. Stir in the salt and tamarind paste.

Heat the peanut oil in a medium skillet over medium heat, add the peanuts, and fry until deeply golden. Watch them as they burn easily. Using a slotted spoon, scoop the peanuts out into a bowl. Turn the heat to high, add the eggs, and fry for 2 minutes (the yolks should be runny).

Using a small bowl, scoop some rice into it and flip it onto a plate. Serve with the fried egg, crispy peanuts, a small bowl of the sambal, and the cucumber and anchovies on the side.

FEEDING FRIENDSHIPS

56 FEEDING FRIENDSHIPS

Olive, orzo, and feta bake

Serves: 2
Prep Time: 10 minutes
Cook Time: 20 minutes

When cooking for a friend or loved one, sometimes you just want to bake or roast something in the oven with minimal effort, so this is why I love a traybake. Here, I use orzo, which is a pasta that is a little larger than rice. It is perfect for a midweek vegetarian meal.

7 ounces (200 g) orzo
3 garlic cloves, sliced
7 ounces (200 g) cherry tomatoes, halved
2 tablespoons olive oil, plus extra for drizzling (optional)
1 cup (100 g) green olives, pitted
1 tablespoon dried oregano
1⅔ cups (400 ml) vegetable stock
⅔ cup (100 g) crumbled feta
1 lemon, sliced into rounds
1 handful of mint, parsley, and dill leaves

Preheat the oven to 400°F (200°C).

Add the orzo, garlic, cherry tomatoes, and olive oil to a 4 by 12-inch (10 by 30 cm) high-sided baking sheet and toss it all together. Stir in the olives and oregano.

Pour the stock into a pot and bring to a boil. Pour the hot stock over the orzo and top with the feta. Finish with the lemon slices and bake in the oven for 20 minutes, or until the orzo is al dente and the feta is brown.

Scoop into bowls and top with herbs and a drizzle of olive oil, if desired.

Chinese poached chicken with ginger dipping oil and steamed rice

This is my speedy version of a classic Chinese dish called Hainanese chicken. This simple poached chicken is transformed when you dunk each bite in the flavorful dipping oil.

Serves: 2
Prep Time: 5 minutes
Cook Time: 20 minutes

4½ cups (1 L) chicken stock
1 lemongrass stalk
4 star anise
1 white onion, halved and skin on
2 boneless chicken breasts, about 6 ounces (170 g) each, skin-on
1 cup (200 g) jasmine rice
2 tablespoons white miso paste
¼ cucumber, sliced on the bias

FOR THE GINGER DIPPING OIL

1 small bunch of cilantro, stems and leaves chopped
1 bunch of scallions, finely chopped
1½-inch (4 cm) piece of ginger, peeled and grated
1 garlic clove, finely chopped
1 green chile, finely chopped
Scant ½ cup (100 ml) peanut oil
1 tablespoon rice wine vinegar
Salt

Pour the stock into a medium pot, add the lemongrass, star anise, and onion, and bring to a gentle simmer. Add the chicken and poach for 20 minutes, making sure the water doesn't boil.

Meanwhile, cook the rice according to the packet directions.

For the dipping oil, add the cilantro, scallions, ginger, garlic, and chile to a heatproof bowl. Heat the oil in a small saucepan until sizzling hot. Test the oil by dipping a chopstick into the pan, and if it sizzles, it is ready. Pour the hot oil into the bowl and let it sizzle away. Season with salt and add the vinegar. Set aside.

Once the chicken is done, remove from the pot and let rest. Scoop out the ingredients in the pot and discard, leaving the broth behind. Add the miso and whisk until dissolved.

Ladle the broth into two serving bowls, scoop the rice onto two plates, and distribute the dipping oil between two small dipping dishes.

Cut the chicken into slices and arrange next to the rice on the plates with the cucumber. Serve.

FEEDING FRIENDSHIPS 59

Crispy fried whole eggplant with tomato sauce

Serves: 2
Prep Time: 6 minutes
Cook Time: 40 minutes

2 medium eggplants
⅔ cup (160 ml) olive oil
1 onion, diced
3 garlic cloves, sliced
1 (14-ounce / 400 g) can chopped tomatoes
Juice of ½ lemon
2⅓ cups (100 g) panko breadcrumbs
¾ cup (100 g) all-purpose flour
2 large eggs
1 handful of basil, plus extra for the topping
2 handfuls of arugula
¼ cup (20 g) grated Parmesan
Salt and pepper

Eggplant parmigiana has a soft spot in my heart. The gooey, slow-roasted, layered eggplant in a tomato sauce and a crispy layer on top is a winning combination. The eggplants can be roasted ahead of time, and the sauce can also be made in advance.

Preheat the oven to 425°F (220°C).

Arrange the whole eggplants on a baking sheet and cook them in the oven for 30 minutes, turning every 10 minutes until the skin is blackened and they are soft.

Meanwhile, make the tomato sauce. Heat 2 tablespoons of the olive oil in a medium saucepan over medium heat, add the onion, and fry, stirring frequently, for 8 minutes. Add the garlic and fry until the garlic is lightly browned.

Add the chopped tomatoes and reduce the heat to a low. Add 1 teaspoon of salt and the lemon juice. Reduce the heat and let simmer.

Meanwhile, add the breadcrumbs to a wide bowl, then add the flour to another wide bowl and season well with salt and pepper. Whisk the eggs in a third wide bowl. Set aside.

Once the eggplants are done, remove them from the oven and let cool enough to handle. Using a fork, carefully remove the skin, making sure to keep the top of the eggplant attached; this will act as a handle.

Pour the remaining olive oil into a large skillet and place over medium heat.

Squash the eggplant out slightly on a clean cutting board, then dip the eggplant, one at a time, first into the flour, then the egg, and finally, the breadcrumbs, until they are evenly coated.

Carefully lower the eggplant into the hot oil and fry for a few minutes, or until golden and crisp. Using a spatula, carefully flip it over and fry it on the other side.

Tear the basil into the tomato sauce and remove from the heat. Spoon the tomato sauce onto two plates, and slide an eggplant onto each plate. Top with a good handful of arugula, extra basil, and finish with grated Parmesan. Serve.

Vegetable fritti with 'nduja aioli

Serves: 2
Prep Time: 2 minutes
Cook Time: 10 minutes

These crispy deep-fried vegetables dunked into the spicy aioli are the perfect combination served with an ice-cold beer on a summer's evening with a friend. If you don't eat 'nduja, swap it for a good-quality harissa paste instead.

2 cups (480 ml) vegetable oil, for frying
¾ cup (100 g) rice flour
½ cup plus 5 teaspoons (80 g) all-purpose flour
1 teaspoon baking powder
½ teaspoon superfine sugar
1 cup (240 ml) cold sparkling water
1 pound (450 g) mixed vegetables, such as purple sprouting broccoli, green beans, and asparagus; cut any large florets in half
1 large handful of sage leaves
Salt and pepper
1 lemon, chopped, for serving

FOR THE AIOLI
3 tablespoons mayonnaise
1 tablespoon 'nduja
1 garlic clove, grated
Zest and juice of ½ lemon
½ bunch of parsley, finely chopped
Salt

Heat the vegetable oil in a large, deep pot or deep-fryer over medium-low heat until it reaches 350°F (180°C) on a thermometer.

Meanwhile, for the aioli, add the mayonnaise, 'nduja, garlic, lemon zest and juice, and parsley to a bowl and mix well. Taste and season with salt. Chill in the refrigerator until needed.

Add ½ cup (70 g) of rice flour, the all-purpose flour, baking powder, and sugar to a medium bowl and whisk briefly together.

Slowly pour the sparkling water into the flour mixture, mixing and whisking as you go until it is a smooth, almost thin batter. It should be the consistency of heavy cream.

Add all the vegetables and sage leaves to a large bowl, along with the remaining ¼ cup (30 g) of rice flour, and using your hands, toss until the vegetables are lightly coated.

Line a baking sheet with paper towels.

Working in batches, dunk the vegetables into the batter and carefully lower them into the hot oil. Deep-fry for a few minutes, turning occasionally until lightly golden and very crisp. Remove with a slotted spoon onto the lined baking sheet and continue until all the vegetables are fried.

Season generously with salt and pepper, and serve with the aioli and a lemon wedge.

FEEDING FRIENDSHIPS 63

64   FEEDING FRIENDSHIPS

Caramelized squash with whipped feta

Serves: 2
Prep Time: 5 minutes
Cook Time: 35 minutes

This sticky, spiced, caramelized squash with whipped creamy feta is a dreamy warm vegetarian meal. This is best made when squash is in season in the fall. You can roast the squash and make the whipped feta in advance, then all you need to do is assemble it at the last minute before serving.

1 small acorn squash, or squash of your choice
1 head of garlic, halved
2 red onions, cut into 8 wedges
3 tablespoons olive oil
½ teaspoon ground cinnamon
1 red chile, thinly sliced
1 tablespoon honey
1 tablespoon za'atar
1 unwaxed lemon, diced, skin and all
1 tablespoon honey
1 handful of mint and parsley leaves
⅓ cup (50 g) chopped toasted pistachios
Salt and pepper

FOR THE WHIPPED FETA
1 (½-pound / 225 g) block of feta
1 tablespoon olive oil
¾ cup (170 g) whole Greek yogurt

Preheat the oven to 400°F (200°C). Cut the squash in half, scoop out the seeds, and discard, then slice the squash into crescent shapes. Spread the squash out on a large baking sheet with the garlic and onions and drizzle with 1 tablespoon of the olive oil. Season well with salt and pepper and roast for 20 minutes.

Meanwhile, add the remaining olive oil to a small bowl. Add the cinnamon, chile, honey, za'atar, and diced lemon, stir well, and set aside.

After 20 minutes, remove the squash from the oven and toss it into the spice mix. Mix well, then remove half of the roasted garlic and set aside. Return the squash to the oven for another 15 minutes.

For the whipped feta, add the feta, olive oil, and yogurt to a blender. Squeeze in the roasted garlic, discarding the skin, and blend until smooth.

Spoon the whipped feta onto a platter. When the squash is ready, arrange on top of the feta, making to scrape up all the crispy bits from the bottom of the baking sheet. Finish with the herbs and chopped pistachios and serve.

Pan pizza

Pizza is very personal. This recipe makes two pan pizzas, but the toppings are only a guide, so add all the ingredients that you love and serve with a peppery green salad. I use a stand mixer to make the dough, but if you don't have one, then simply knead by hand.

Serves: 2
Prep Time: 15 minutes + rising
Cook Time: 45 minutes

FOR THE DOUGH

1½ cups (360 ml) lukewarm water
¼-ounce (7 g) active dry yeast
3⅓ cups (450 g) strong white bread flour
1 teaspoon unrefined superfine sugar
1 teaspoon salt
2 tablespoons olive oil, plus extra for drizzling
3 tablespoons coarse semolina

FOR THE TOMATO SAUCE

3½ tablespoons olive oil
2 garlic cloves, sliced
1 (14-ounce / 400 g) can chopped tomatoes
1 handful of basil leaves

FOR THE TOPPINGS

8 anchovy filets from a tin in olive oil
2 tablespoons capers, drained
2 broccoli florets, thinly sliced
1 (5½-ounce / 160 g) ball of mozzarella
1¾ ounces (50 g) spicy pepperoni
3 pickled hot chiles, sliced
1 cup (100 g) grated Parmesan
1 pinch of red pepper flakes
1 tablespoon spicy honey
1 handful of basil leaves

For the dough, pour the lukewarm water into a stand mixer fitted with a dough hook, add the yeast, and let stand for 5 minutes until the yeast is bubbly and foamy. Tip in the flour, sugar, and salt, then add the olive oil and mix on medium speed until it is smooth and elastic, 6 minutes. Cover the bowl with a damp dish towel and let rise in a warm place until doubled in size.

Meanwhile, for the sauce, heat the olive oil in a medium saucepan over medium heat. Add the garlic and fry until lightly golden. Add the tomatoes, bring to a simmer, and cook until thick, 20 minutes. Remove the pan from the heat, tear in the basil, and set aside.

Preheat the oven to 425°F (220°C).

Once the dough has risen, divide it into two equal pieces. Spread the semolina out on a plate.

Drizzle two 10-inch (25 cm) ovenproof pans well with olive oil. Dip the dough balls into the semolina, then, using your hands, stretch the dough out in the pan, pushing it up the sides as you go.

Top the doughs with tomato sauce, then one with anchovies, capers, sliced broccoli, and half the mozzarella, and the other with pepperoni, guindilla chiles, and the remaining mozzarella. Sprinkle both with grated Parmesan.

Fry the pizzas over high heat for a few minutes, then transfer them to the oven and bake on the bottom shelf for 20 minutes.

Carefully remove the pizzas from the oven and slide them out onto a plate. Top the pepperoni pizza with red pepper flakes and a drizzle of spicy honey, and sprinkle basil over both pizzas. Cut into slices and serve.

Watermelon, feta, and za'atar salad

Serves: 2
Prep Time: 10 minutes

This dish comes together quickly and is perfect in the summer when watermelon is at its best. Serve with some crusty bread to dunk in, if desired.

1 small watermelon, about 3¼ pounds (1.5 kg)
⅖ cup (60 g) Kalamata olives, pitted and chopped
1 tablespoon za'atar
Zest and juice of 1 lemon
3 tablespoons olive oil
1 red onion, sliced
½ cucumber, sliced
1 handful of cherry tomatoes, halved
1 handful of each mint and parsley leaves
3½ ounces (100 g) feta
Salt and pepper

Using a sharp knife, slice off the ends of the watermelon, then stand the melon upright, slice the outer skin off, and discard. Once peeled, chop the flesh into irregular bite-size shapes and set aside.

Add the chopped olives, za'atar, and lemon zest and juice to a salad bowl and pour over the olive oil. Season to taste with salt and pepper.

Add the watermelon, red onion, cucumber, cherry tomatoes, and herbs to the bowl and mix well until everything is coated.

Crumble over the feta and serve.

FEEDING FRIENDSHIPS 69

FEEDING FRIENDSHIPS

Whipped tahini and Brussels sprout salad

Serves: 2
Prep Time: 10 minutes
Cook Time: 20 minutes

If you have never had whipped tahini before, you are in for a treat. The sweet-roasted Brussels sprouts against the cooling, tangy tahini is so good. Serve with charred flatbreads, a warm salad, and crispy chicken thighs, although it's delicious without chicken, too.

½ red onion, diced
Juice of 1½ lemons, divided
3½ ounces (100 g) raw kale
1 pound (450 g) Brussels sprouts, halved
¾ cup (100 g) chopped dates
2 tablespoons olive oil
4 boneless chicken thighs, skin-on
1 cup (225 g) tahini
1 garlic clove, peeled but left whole
¾ cup (180 ml) water
¾ cup (80 g) toasted pecans
2 shallots, diced
Salt

Preheat the oven to 425°F (220°C).

Add the diced onion to a large bowl. Squeeze in the juice of one lemon, and add a large pinch of salt. Add the kale and, using your hands, give everything a good mix until the kale starts to feel a little soft and the onions turn bright pink.

Add the Brussels sprouts, dates, and olive oil to a separate bowl and season well with salt. Tip onto a large baking sheet and turn the Brussels sprouts over so they are all cut-side down. Roast in the oven for 20 minutes.

Season the chicken really well with salt and place it in a cold skillet. Place the skillet over medium heat and fry the chicken until golden on one side, 8 minutes.

Meanwhile, for the whipped tahini, blend the tahini, garlic, the remaining lemon juice, ½ teaspoon of salt, and the water in a blender until smooth and thickened, about 3 minutes.

Turn the chicken over and fry for another 6 minutes, or until cooked through. Remove and let rest for a few minutes before slicing.

When the Brussels sprouts are ready, spread the sauce thinly across a platter and top with the roasted Brussels sprouts and dates, including all the juices from the sheet. Add the kale, onions, and pecans, then top with the chicken and serve.

Spinach, feta, and herb pie with labneh and Turkish chile butter

Serves: 2
Prep Time: 5 minutes
Cook Time: 30 minutes

This is an amalgamation of everything I love in phyllo pastry from my journeys in Greece and Turkey. Its vibrant green filling is packed full of goodness and there is something about eating crispy, buttery phyllo with the spiced labneh that is a combo you can't miss. If you can't purchase labneh, you can either make your own or simply use very thick Greek yogurt. Serve with a salad of chopped tomatoes, cucumber, and red onions.

7 tablespoons (100 g) melted butter
8 phyllo pastry sheets
1 teaspoon nigella seeds
1 handful of dill, for garnish

FOR THE FILLING
3⅓ cups (200 g) coarsely chopped spinach
1⅓ cups (200 g) crumbled feta
Zest of 1 lemon
¾ cup (20 g) finely chopped dill
¾ cup (20 g) chopped parsley
¾ cup (100 g) chopped toasted pistachios
3 eggs

FOR THE LABNEH
¾ cup (180 g) labneh
3½ tablespoons butter
½ teaspoon Aleppo pepper
½ teaspoon sumac

Preheat the oven to 400°F (200°C).

For the filling, place a large skillet over high heat, add the spinach, and stir until just wilted. Tip the spinach into a clean dish towel and squeeze out the moisture. Add the spinach to a bowl with the feta, lemon zest, dill, parsley, and pistachios, and mix. Add the eggs and mix again until combined.

Brush the melted butter over an 8-inch (20 cm) round ovenproof skillet and drape a sheet of phyllo over the top, letting the excess hang over the side of the pan. Add the remaining sheets in layers, brushing with butter as you go and moving the sheets around as you layer.

Pour in the filling and fold the excess phyllo over the top to create a lid. Brush with the remaining butter. Place the pan over medium heat and fry for 5 minutes. Sprinkle over the nigella seeds. Transfer to the oven and bake on the bottom shelf for 25 minutes until golden. Carefully remove the pie from the oven, slide it onto a board, and let stand for 1 minute.

Add the labneh to a heatproof bowl. Melt the butter in a small pan with the Aleppo pepper and sumac, and let bubble a little until the butter has turned lightly golden, then drizzle it over the labneh. Garnish the pie with dill and serve with the labneh.

FEEDING FRIENDSHIPS

Vodka and gochujang pasta

Serves: 2
Prep Time: 5 minutes
Cook Time: 30 minutes

2 tablespoons olive oil
1 onion, finely diced
4 garlic cloves, minced
2 tablespoons gochujang paste
¼ cup (60 g) tomato paste
½ teaspoon red pepper flakes
2 tablespoons vodka
¾ cup (180 ml) heavy cream
12 ounces (340 g) Calamarata or rigatoni pasta
2 tablespoons unsalted butter
¼ cup (20 g) grated Parmesan, plus extra for serving
Flaky sea salt and pepper

If you are like me and love a spicy kick to your pasta, then this is for you. The smoky gochujang and cream balance each other out. This is now a classic Korean American fusion dish in my eyes, and it's a simple hug in a bowl.

Heat the olive oil in a large heavy pot over medium heat. Add the onion, garlic, and 1 teaspoon of salt and fry until softened and the edges of the onion begins to brown, 6 minutes.

Add the gochujang, tomato paste, and red pepper flakes to the pot and cook, stirring frequently, for 6 minutes, or until the mixture is quite dry, thick, and has turned a dark amber color. Pour in the vodka and cook for another 1 minute, scraping up any crispy bits from the bottom of the pot. Turn off the heat and pour in the cream.

Bring a large pot of water to a boil. Season with salt, then add the pasta and cook according to the packet directions, or until al dente. Drain the pasta, setting a mugful of the pasta cooking water aside.

Tip the pasta into the sauce and place it over low heat. Add the butter and Parmesan and stir, moving the pasta around until the butter has melted. Pour in half of the reserved pasta water and keep stirring until it is a smooth shiny sauce. You may not need all the water.

Divide the pasta between two bowls, top with extra Parmesan and lots of pepper, and serve.

FEEDING FRIENDSHIPS

DATE

NIGHTS

DATE NIGHTS

Steamed whole fish finished with a sizzling scallion oil

Serves: 2
Prep Time: 10 minutes
Cook Time: 12 minutes

Serving a whole steamed fish to someone special feels impressive, and this simple dish will impress on all levels. To steam the fish, place it on a platter, then sit it on a trivet in a wok with a lid. While steaming, make sure that the water doesn't dry out. You can also use a steamer or a steam basket in a large pot.

1 bunch of scallions, green and white parts very thinly sliced separately
1 teaspoon sugar
1 tablespoon Shaoxing wine
2 tablespoons light soy sauce
1 teaspoon sesame oil
1 tablespoon water
1 (2-pound / 900 g) whole cleaned and gutted sea bream
¼ teaspoon ground white pepper
1½-inch (4 cm) piece of ginger, peeled and very thinly sliced
Salt
1 bunch of cilantro, for garnish
Steamed rice of your choice, for serving

FOR THE HOT OIL

Scant ½ cup (100 ml) peanut oil
4 garlic cloves, sliced
1 red chile, sliced on the bias

Place the green parts of the scallions in a bowl of ice-cold water so they curl up.

In a small bowl, mix the sugar, Shaoxing wine, soy sauce, sesame oil, and water together.

Using a sharp knife, slash three equal slits into the fish. Season inside and out with salt and the white pepper, then lay the fish on a platter and cover the fish in the wine and soy sauce mixture. Top with half of the ginger. Transfer the fish to a steamer and steam for 12 minutes.

For the hot oil, add the peanut oil to a small saucepan with the garlic, the remaining ginger, the chile, and the white parts of the scallions. Fry, stirring frequently, until the garlic and ginger are golden and crisp, 5 to 6 minutes.

When the fish is ready, carefully transfer the fish to a serving dish. Pour the hot oil over, then garnish with cilantro and serve with rice.

Beef wellington with horseradish spinach

Serves: 2
Prep Time: 10 minutes
Cook Time: 45 minutes

This two-person wellington is perfect when trying to impress someone special, especially if served by candlelight with a delicious bottle of red wine. You can prepare the wellington the day before, then just remove it from the refrigerator 30 minutes before cooking. This dish may look a little tricky, but it's simple.

10 ounces (280 g) mixed mushrooms
3 banana shallots, peeled but left whole
2 garlic cloves, peeled but left whole
4 tablespoons olive oil
1 tablespoon dried thyme
1 tablespoon balsamic vinegar
3 rosemary sprigs, leaves picked and finely chopped
¾ pound (340 g) beef tenderloin (you want a nice even size piece)
8 sheets of prosciutto
1 tablespoon English mustard
1 (11-ounce / 320 g) all-butter puff pastry sheet
1 tablespoon all-purpose flour, for dusting
1 large egg, beaten
Flaky sea salt
Store-bought gravy, for serving
Dijon mustard, for serving

FOR THE SPINACH

3½ tablespoons salted butter
4 cups (200 g) baby spinach
Juice of ½ lemon
2 tablespoons creamed horseradish

Pulse the mushrooms, shallots, and garlic in a food processor until it is all very finely diced.

Place a large skillet over high heat, add 2 tablespoons of the oil, then tip in the mushroom mix and fry until all the water has cooked out and the mushrooms are drying out, 10 minutes.

Add the thyme and vinegar and fry for another 2 minutes. Remove from the heat, scoop onto a plate, and let cool. Wipe the skillet clean and place back over high heat.

Mix the rosemary and 1 heaping teaspoon of salt together on a clean counter, then roll the beef in the flavored salt. Pour 1 tablespoon of the oil into the hot skillet, add the beef, and fry until well seared on all sides, 5 minutes. Remove and set aside.

Preheat the oven to 375°F (190°C). Oil a large baking sheet with the remaining oil.

Place a large sheet of plastic wrap on a counter and lay the prosciutto neatly over each other, creating a flat layer.

Spread the English mustard evenly over the prosciutto, then spread the mushroom pâté over in an even layer, leaving a ½-inch (1 cm) border. Place the beef in the center, then gather up the plastic wrap and twist into a package.

Unroll the pastry sheet on a lightly floured counter and slice in half. Unwrap the beef and place it in the middle of one-half of the pastry sheet. Using a pastry brush, brush the edges around the beef with beaten egg, then drape over the remaining piece of pastry to cover and press to seal. Trim the excess pastry and crimp the edges.

Transfer the wellington to the greased baking sheet and brush the remaining beaten egg all over. Using a butter knife, lightly make crisscross lines across one side and then the other, making sure to be light so you don't pierce the pastry.

Cook the wellington on the bottom shelf of the oven until the pastry is golden on top and crisp underneath, 35 minutes.

Remove the wellington and let rest for 5 minutes while you prepare the spinach.

Melt the butter in a large skillet over medium heat until it starts to go a light golden color. Tip in the spinach and squeeze over the lemon juice. Fry until wilted, then continue to fry until the water has evaporated. Add the horseradish and fry for another 30 seconds. Remove the skillet from the heat.

Cut the wellington into slices and serve with the spinach, gravy, and a dollop of Dijon mustard.

Pasta alla vongole

Serves: 2
Prep Time: 5 minutes
Cook Time: 10 minutes

This classic southern Italian pasta is my favorite pasta recipe of all time. This dish is really quick to make so you need all your preparation done before you start cooking.

10 ounces (280 g) dried spaghetti
⅓ cup (80 ml) extra-virgin olive oil
2 banana shallots, thinly sliced
3 garlic cloves, thinly sliced
1 small bunch of parsley, stems thinly sliced and leaves coarsely chopped
10 cherry tomatoes, quartered
¼ teaspoon red pepper flakes
Juice of 1 lemon
1 cup (240 ml) white wine
1½ pounds (680 g) small clams, scrubbed clean
Salt and pepper

Bring a large pot of water to a boil. Season with salt, add the pasta, and cook according to the package directions, or until al dente.

Once the spaghetti has been cooking for 2 minutes, start the sauce. Heat the oil in a large saucepan with a tight-fitting lid over medium heat. Add the shallots and garlic and fry until lightly golden.

Add the parsley stems, tomatoes, and red pepper flakes. Add the lemon juice and fry for another minute. Pour in half of the wine and cook for a few minutes until the wine has evaporated. Tip in the cleaned clams and pour in the remaining wine. It will splutter, so be careful. Shake well, and then cover with the lid. After about 3 or 4 minutes, the clams will start to open, so keep shaking the pan around until all of them have opened. Remove the pan from the heat and discard any clams that are still closed.

The pasta should be perfectly al dente now, so drain and add the pasta to the clams. Add the parsley leaves and season to taste with salt and pepper. Serve.

DATE NIGHTS

Spiced green risotto

Serves: 2
Prep Time: 10 minutes
Cook Time: 45 minutes

This risotto is based on one I ate while I was in Sicily. Try to find small pale green bell peppers as they work best in this dish, but if you can't get them, then use eight smaller Turkish peppers instead.

FOR THE RISOTTO

3⅓ cups (800 ml) vegetable or chicken stock
2 tablespoons extra-virgin olive oil
1 white onion, finely chopped
2 garlic cloves, finely chopped
¾ cup (150 g) risotto rice
¾ cup (180 ml) white wine
3½ tablespoons salted butter
Salt and pepper

FOR THE PESTO

4 small pale green bell peppers
2 long green chiles
⅔ cup (75 g) shelled, toasted pistachios, plus extra chopped for garnish
1 garlic clove, peeled but left whole
Juice of 1 lemon
Scant ½ cup (100 ml) extra-virgin olive oil
2 cups (50 g) basil leaves, plus 1 small handful for the top
⅓ cup (30 g) grated pecorino or Parmesan

For the pesto, char the peppers and chiles over an open flame on the stove or under a preheated broiler until the skin is blackened all over. You can also do this on a barbecue. Transfer the peppers to a bowl, cover with a plate or lid, and let cool.

Meanwhile, for the risotto, heat the stock in a medium pot over low heat until hot. Keep it over the heat to stay warm.

Heat a medium heavy saucepan over medium heat, add the olive oil and onion, and fry until the onion is soft, 10 minutes. Add the garlic and cook for 2 minutes.

Increase the heat to high, add the rice and a little more oil if needed and toast on all sides until the rice has turned slightly translucent, 5 minutes.

Pour in the wine and let evaporate, stirring as it does. Ladle in a ladleful of the hot stock and stir until it evaporates, then continue this process until all the stock is used. This should take about 15 to 20 minutes. The rice is perfectly cooked when it is al dente. When you break a grain of rice with your fingers, you should be able to see a tiny fleck of white in the middle. Reduce the heat to low while you finish making the pesto.

The peppers should be cool enough to handle now. Using your hands, peel the charred skin off the peppers, discarding the blackened skin. Tear the peppers open and discard the seeds. Put the peppers into a blender, then add the pistachios, garlic, lemon juice, olive oil, basil leaves, and half the grated pecorino and blend until it is smooth and a vivid green color.

Add the butter and half of the leftover pecorino to the risotto. Season to taste with salt and pepper and stir vigorously. Cover the risotto with a lid and let stand for 5 minutes.

Stir the pesto through the risotto. If the risotto looks a little thick, add a little more hot stock or boiling water.

Top with the remaining cheese, a handful of basil leaves, and a few chopped pistachios. Serve.

Lady and the tramp spaghetti and meatballs with a spiced tomato sauce

There is nothing more romantic than the idea of eating pasta with a loved one by candlelight at a well-dressed table with a bottle of good-quality red wine. It's a winning combination all round.

Serves: 2
Prep Time: 10 minutes
Cook Time: 45 minutes

9 ounces (255 g) dried spaghetti
⅓ cup (30 g) grated Parmesan
1 handful of basil leaves
Salt

FOR THE MEATBALLS
1¾ ounces (50 g) stale white bread, crusts removed and coarsely torn into chunks
⅓ cup (80 ml) whole milk
10 ounces (280 g) ground pork, 10% fat
½ teaspoon fennel seeds
½ teaspoon red pepper flakes
½ teaspoon dried oregano
1 tablespoon extra-virgin olive oil

FOR THE SAUCE
1 white onion, peeled but left whole
1 small celery stalk, peeled
1 small carrot, peeled
2½ tablespoons extra-virgin olive oil
3 garlic cloves, thinly sliced
1 teaspoon red pepper flakes
1 pinch of ground cinnamon
2 cups (480 ml) strained canned tomatoes (passata)
1 teaspoon sugar

For the meatballs, place the bread chunks in a medium bowl. Pour over the milk and let stand.

Meanwhile, for the tomato sauce, pulse the onion, celery, and carrot in a blender until everything is very finely chopped.

Pour the olive oil into a wide heavy pan and place over medium heat. Add the garlic and fry for 2 minutes, then add the chopped vegetables and fry, stirring frequently, for 10 minutes.

Add the red pepper flakes and cinnamon and fry for another 1 minute. Pour in the tomatoes and season with 1 teaspoon of salt and the sugar. Reduce the heat and simmer for 20 minutes.

Meanwhile, for the meatballs, add the pork to a large bowl and season generously with salt. Add the fennel seeds, red pepper flakes, and oregano.

Using clean hands, squeeze the bread to remove any excess milk, then add to the pork mixture and mix thoroughly with your hands until combined. Form the meat mixture into eight walnut-size meatballs.

Place a large skillet over high heat and add the olive oil. Add the meatballs and fry until they are golden all over, 6 minutes. Tip the meatballs and any juices from the pan into the tomato sauce.

Bring a large saucepan of water to a boil. Season with salt, add the pasta, and cook according to the package directions, or until al dente. Drain the pasta, tip it into the tomato sauce, and stir until the pasta is evenly coated in the sauce.

Spoon the pasta and meatballs into bowls and top with grated Parmesan and basil leaves.

Sesame-crusted seared tuna with a crispy garlic and chile salad

Serves: 2
Prep Time: 5 minutes
Cook Time: 10 minutes

This sesame-crusted tuna is a beauty to look at. It is light yet filling, and is perfect when trying to impress. Serve with cold sake, if desired. Make sure to buy sushi-grade tuna. Shiso leaves are also called Chinese basil or perilla mint and are popular in Japanese cuisine. Buy it in specialty Asian stores.

FOR THE TUNA
2 (8½-ounce / 240 g) sushi-grade yellowfin tuna steaks
1 tablespoon toasted sesame oil
⅓ cup (50 g) mixed sesame seeds

FOR THE CRISPY SALAD
4 scallions, halved in the middle, then lengthwise, then thinly sliced into matchsticks
2 tablespoons peanut or vegetable oil
4 garlic cloves, thinly sliced
2 red chiles, thinly sliced diagonally
½ cup (60 g) chopped raw cashews
1 handful of cilantro leaves
1 handful of shiso leaves
1 ripe avocado, peeled, pitted, and cut into slices
1 jalapeño chile, sliced, for garnish

FOR THE DRESSING
Juice of 1 lime
Juice of ½ orange
2 tablespoons ponzu
1 tablespoon soy sauce
1 teaspoon sesame oil

Start with the crispy salad. Place the scallions in a bowl of ice-cold water so they curl up.

Line a plate with paper towels. Heat the oil in a small wok or skillet over medium heat, add the garlic and chiles, and fry until crisp and the garlic is almost golden. Add the cashews and fry until golden. Tip out onto the lined plate and set aside.

Rub the tuna steaks with the sesame oil. Spread the mixed sesame seeds out onto a plate, then roll the tuna steaks, one at a time, around in them until both steaks are fully coated.

Heat a large skillet over high heat until very hot. Add the tuna and fry for 2 minutes on each side. Remove from the pan and let stand.

For the dressing, add the lime juice, orange juice, ponzu, soy sauce, and sesame oil to a bowl and stir to combine.

Add the cilantro and shiso leaves to a platter, with the avocado. Sprinkle over the crispy garlic, chiles, and cashews.

Slice the tuna steaks into ¼-inch (5 mm) slices and lay over the salad. Drizzle the dressing over the top. Drain the scallions and add them to the salad with the jalapeño as a garnish.

DATE NIGHTS 89

Corn chowder and seared scallops

Serves: 2
Prep Time: 10 minutes
Cook Time: 30 minutes

This chowder is decadent and vibrant. You can make the chowder ahead of time, then simply fry the scallops and toppings when you are ready to eat. Serve with crusty bread for a more substantial meal.

3½ ounces (100 g) bacon lardons
1 tablespoon butter
1 leek, finely sliced
2 garlic cloves, finely sliced
Pinch of red pepper flakes
7 ounces (200 g) cauliflower, cut into small florets
4 corn on the cobs, kernels sliced off the husk (about 4¼ cups / 650 g kernels)
1⅔ cups (400 ml) chicken stock
¾ cup (180 ml) white wine
Juice of ½ lemon
⅔ cup (160 ml) heavy cream
Salt and pepper
1 green chile, thinly sliced, for garnish
1 small handful of sliced chives, for garnish

FOR THE SCALLOPS
1 tablespoon butter
1 tablespoon olive oil
6 medium scallops, cleaned
¼ cup (60 g) chopped blanched almonds

Fry the bacon in a heavy saucepan over medium heat until golden and crisp, 6 minutes. Remove the bacon from the pan and set aside, leaving the fat behind.

Add the butter, sliced leek, and a good pinch of salt, and fry for 10 minutes, or until the leek is soft and sticky.

Add the garlic and red pepper flakes and cook for 2 minutes, then add the cauliflower florets and all but a handful of the corn kernels. Pour in the stock, wine, and lemon juice, then simmer for 20 minutes.

Once the chowder has thickened and the cauliflower is very soft to the touch, blend half with a stick blender. Leave the pan over low heat and pour in the cream. Season to taste with salt and pepper.

For the scallops, heat the butter and oil in a medium skillet until bubbling and foamy. Add the scallops and fry for 1½ minutes on one side. Using tongs, turn the scallops over, add the reserved corn kernels, bacon, and almonds and fry for another 1½ minutes.

Remove the scallops from the pan and season with salt and pepper. Continue to fry corn, bacon, and almonds for another minute.

Ladle the chowder into shallow bowls, top with the scallops, spoon over the bacon mixture and garnish with the chile and chives.

DATE NIGHTS 91

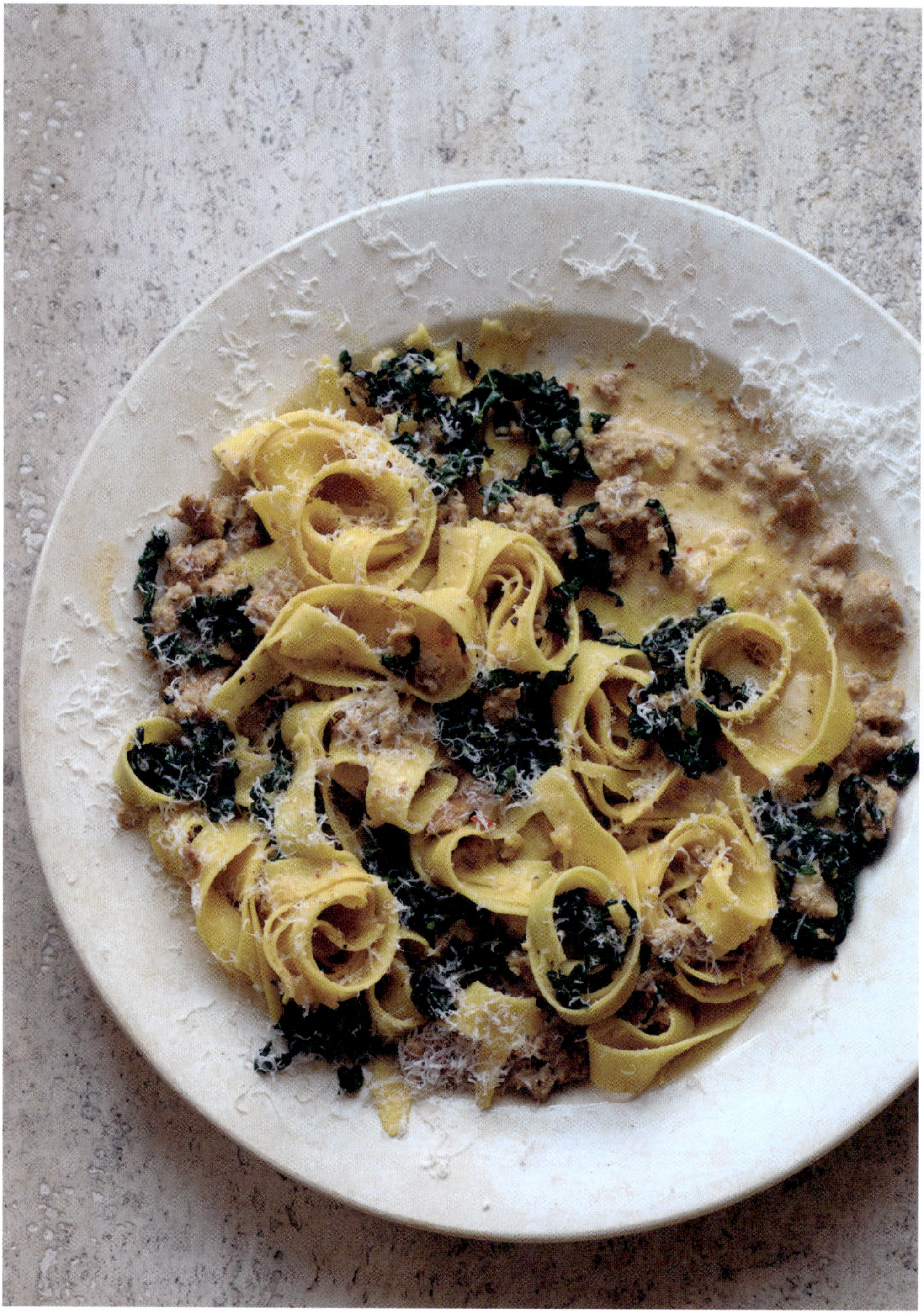

Pork sausage and fennel tagliatelle

Serves: 2
Prep Time: 10 minutes
Cook Time: 55 minutes

There is something about a white ragù peppered with fennel that will always be special. It is much quicker to make than a beef ragù, but is still punchy in flavor. I like my ragù spicy, but if you aren't a fan, simply leave out the red pepper flakes.

10 ounces (280 g) good-quality Italian sausages
1 small onion, finely diced
1 head of fennel, finely diced
2 garlic cloves, grated
1 rosemary stalk, leaves picked and chopped
1 tablespoon olive oil
1 teaspoon fennel seeds
1 teaspoon red pepper flakes, or to taste
⅔ cup (160 ml) white wine
⅔ cup (160 ml) heavy cream
⅔ cup (160 ml) chicken stock
7 ounces (200 g) fresh egg tagliatelle
⅔ cup (60 g) grated Parmesan
Salt and pepper

Slit the skins of the sausages and squeeze the meat out into a wide pan with a lid. Place over medium heat and fry for 10 minutes, or until the fat has rendered and the meat is turning golden, breaking the meat up with a wooden spoon occasionally. Add the onion, fennel, garlic, rosemary, and olive oil.

Bash the fennel seeds in a mortar and pestle, add the red pepper flakes, and cook, stirring frequently, for 10 minutes. Pour in the wine and cook for 5 minutes.

Add the cream and stock. Season with salt and pepper, then cover the pan with a lid and simmer gently for 30 minutes.

In the last 5 minutes, bring a large saucepan of water to a boil. Season with salt, add the pasta, and cook according to the packet directions, or until al dente.

Remove the ragu from the heat and, using tongs, add the pasta to the sauce, tossing very well. Gently stir in half the cheese and serve with the remaining cheese at the table.

Crispy pork chops with roasted grapes and celery root mash

This pork chop dish is so good, as the roasted grapes go jammy and sticky and become a sweet tangy lift to the whole dish. I like to buy well-reared, good-quality chops.

Serves: 2
Prep Time: 5 minutes
Cook Time: 55 minutes

FOR THE CELERY ROOT MASH
1 medium celery root, about 1 pound (450 g), peeled and cut into ¾-inch (2 cm) chunks
Juice of 1 lemon
¼ cup (60 g) butter
Scant ½ cup (100 ml) heavy cream
1 tablespoon wholegrain mustard
Salt

FOR THE GRAPES
1 small bunch of black seedless grapes on the vine
1 tablespoon olive oil
1 teaspoon honey
1 tablespoon red wine vinegar
Salt

FOR THE CHOPS
2 (1-inch / 2.5 cm) thick bone-in pork chops with skin on
1 tablespoon salted butter
1 tablespoon olive oil
1 handful of sage
Salt

Preheat the oven to 425°F (220°C). Line a baking sheet with wax paper.

Add the celery root to a large pan with a lid. Season with salt, add the lemon juice, and pour in enough boiling water to cover. Bring to a rolling boil, then cover with the lid and simmer until the celery root is soft when prodded with a knife, 20 minutes.

Meanwhile, roast the grapes. Pull the grapes into five small bundles. Arrange them on the lined baking sheet and drizzle over the oil, honey, and vinegar. Season with salt and roast in the oven for 20 minutes.

Meanwhile, for the chops, using a sharp knife, cut the skin away from the fat, leaving half the fat on the skin and half on the chop. Cut the skin into ½-inch (1 cm) strips. Add the skin to a large skillet, place over medium heat, and fry, moving them around occasionally, until you have little crackling bits of pork, 10 minutes.

When the celery root is ready, drain in a colander and add to a blender with the butter and cream. Add a good pinch of salt and blend until smooth. Fold the mustard through, scoop into a pan, and place over low heat.

Season the pork chops well with salt. Remove the crackling from the pan and set aside, leaving the fat behind. Increase the heat under the pan to high and fry the pork fat-side first for a few minutes, or until the fat is golden and crisp. Carefully flip the chops over and fry for a few minutes on each side, or until golden brown. For the last minute, add the butter and oil and fry, basting the chops with the butter. Transfer the chops to a plate and rest for 5 minutes. Add the sage to the pan and fry until crisp.

Coarsely chop the crispy skin and season well with salt.

When ready to serve, divide the celery root between two plates, top with a chop, a couple of bundles of roasted grapes, crispy pork skin, and the sage leaves.

Pasta with fennel, tuna, and Pernod

Serves: 2
Prep time: 10 minutes
Cook time: 30 to 40 minutes

I created this pasta dish when I had an abundance of fennel and it is now my husband's most requested dinner. When fennel is cooked in this way, it becomes sweet. This is a love letter to fennel. Try to buy the more expensive tuna that comes in jars and is seasoned with good-quality olive oil. Pernod is an anise-flavored aperitif from France, which can be found in most grocery stores.

¼ cup (50 g) capers, well-drained
Scant ½ cup (100 ml) olive oil, plus extra for drizzling
2 heads of fennel, trimmed
4 garlic cloves, sliced
1 onion, diced
Zest and juice of 1 lemon
9 ounces (255 g) spaghetti
½ teaspoon fennel seeds
½ teaspoon red pepper flakes
2 (7¾-ounce / 220 g) jars tuna in olive oil, drained
Scant ½ cup (100 ml) Pernod
Salt

Add the capers to a wide, heavy pot and pour in the oil. Place over medium heat and fry until the capers start to pop and go crisp. Once they have gone a darker green and become crispy, remove them with a slotted spoon to a plate, leaving the caper oil behind. Remove the pan from the heat.

Set aside any fennel fronds in a bowl of cold water. Remove the outer layers of the fennel and discard, then finely dice the fennel and add to the caper oil. Add the garlic and onion and place over medium heat. Add the lemon zest and juice and fry, stirring frequently, for 20 minutes, or until everything has become soft and sticky in places and a golden brown color.

Bring a large pan of water to a boil. Season with salt, then add the pasta, and cook according to the packet directions, or until al dente.

Meanwhile, bash the fennel seeds in a mortar and pestle. Add to the pan with the fennel and garlic, then add the red pepper flakes and fry for another 2 minutes. Add the tuna to the pan, then pour over the Pernod and let the alcohol evaporate. Reduce the heat to a low simmer.

When the spaghetti is cooked, drain, setting aside a mugful of the pasta cooking water.

Tip the spaghetti into the tuna and mix very well until everything is combined. Pour in the reserved pasta cooking water and stir until the sauce is glossy and sticky. You may not need all the water. Serve the pasta with the crispy capers, fennel fronds, and a good drizzle of oil.

Confit tomato and caper tart with Parmesan

When tomatoes are in season I make trays of confit and use it for tomato sauce, in salads, and in this simple tart. The oil is also delicious and is perfect for dunking bread in and drizzling over salads. The tomatoes can be cooked in the oven in the morning, then left to cool, so you can make the tart when you are ready. Serve with a bitter leaf salad.

Serves: 2
Prep Time: 5 minutes
Cook Time: 2 hours

2¼ pounds (1 kg) tomatoes, a mix of sizes and shapes, cut large ones in half
1 head garlic, unpeeled and bashed
2 teaspoons kosher sea salt
1 teaspoon fennel seeds
1 teaspoon red pepper flakes
1¼ cups (300 ml) extra-virgin olive oil
Scant ⅓ cup (40 g) grated Parmesan
Zest of 1 lemon
1 (11-ounce / 320 g) all-butter puff pastry sheet
1 handful of basil leaves, for garnish

Preheat the oven to 300°F (150°C).

Add the tomatoes, leaving on any stalks or vines, to a 6 by 12-inch (15 by 30 cm) baking sheet. If the baking sheet is too big, it will affect the amount of oil you need. Add the garlic, salt, and sprinkle over the fennel seeds and red pepper flakes. Pour in the olive oil, making sure it comes two-thirds of the way up the tomatoes. Roast until the tomatoes are sticky and reduced slightly, 1½ hours. Remove the tomatoes from the oven and let cool slightly. Increase the oven temperature to 400°F (200°C).

Once the tomatoes have cooled a little, squeeze out the garlic from its papery skins, discarding the skins, and add to the tomatoes.

Carefully remove the tomatoes and garlic from the oil and set aside. Pour the oil into a sterilized jar. You can use it on everything.

Sprinkle half the Parmesan over the bottom of a heavy skillet, then top with the tomatoes and the lemon zest.

Unroll the puff pastry sheet and drape it over the skillet. Trim into a circle, leaving plenty of pastry hanging over the edges. Using a butter knife, tuck the overhanging pastry into the edges of the skillet, creating a seal around the tomatoes. Cut a small cross in the middle for steam to escape.

Bake in the oven until the pastry is golden, puffed up, and crisp, 20 to 25 minutes.

Remove the tart from the oven, place a cutting board over the skillet, and carefully flip the tart over. Sprinkle with the remaining Parmesan, garnish with basil leaves, and serve.

Greek shrimp and orzo bake

Serves: 2
Prep Time: 10 minutes
Cook Time: 35 to 40 minutes

I first had Greek shrimp saganaki when I was thirteen on a family holiday in Greece and I loved it so much, I still cook it. It is full of Greek flavors that make me long for summer evenings by the sea. Serve with an ice-cold wine and pretend you are in Greece for an evening.

8 large king shrimp, heads and tails on but shell peeled and deveined
Scant ½ cup (100 ml) ouzo
Zest and juice of 1 lemon
1 teaspoon red pepper flakes
3 tablespoons olive oil
2 onions, sliced
1 teaspoon sea salt
4 garlic cloves, diced
2 teaspoons dried Greek oregano
2 tablespoons tomato paste
¾ cup (180 ml) dry white wine
1¼ cups (300 g) chopped cherry tomatoes
10 ounces (280 g) orzo
2 cups (480 ml) hot chicken stock
Scant ½ cup (60 g) crumbled feta
1 handful of dill
1 lemon, cut into wedges, for serving

Preheat the oven to 375°F (190°C).

Combine the shrimp, ouzo, lemon zest and juice, and red pepper flakes in a bowl and set aside.

Heat the olive oil in a medium ovenproof skillet over medium heat. Add the onions and salt, and fry until the onions are softened, 10 minutes. Stir in the garlic, oregano, and tomato paste and cook for 3 minutes. Increase the heat to high and pour in the wine. Add the cherry tomatoes, orzo, and stock.

Transfer the skillet to the oven and bake for 25 minutes. With 3 minutes left of cooking, stir in the shrimp, making sure to add any of the marinade, and bake until the shrimp have turned bright pink and are cooked through.

Once cooked, add the feta and finish with the dill. Serve with lemon wedges.

DATE NIGHTS

Crispy chicken cutlets with olive, tomato, nectarine, and mozzarella salad

This crispy Parmesan-breaded chicken has everything you want on those warmer summer evenings. It looks very pretty and is also flavorsome, so it is ideal when you want to impress someone.

Serves: 2
Prep Time: 15 minutes
Cook Time: 12 minutes

FOR THE CRISPY CHICKEN

3¾ tablespoons all-purpose flour
1 teaspoon garlic powder
1 teaspoon onion powder
1 teaspoon sweet paprika
1 large egg
1 cup (50 g) panko breadcrumbs
1 small bunch of thyme leaves
¼ cup (20 g) grated Parmesan
2 boneless chicken breasts, about 6 ounces (170 g) each
⅔ cup (160 ml) vegetable oil
Salt and pepper

FOR THE SALAD

3 ripe nectarines, halved and pitted
1 handful of green olives, pitted
7 ounces (200 g) mixed cherry tomatoes, halved
½ red onion, diced
Zest and juice of ½ unwaxed lemon
1 small bunch of parsley, chopped
1 (4½-ounce / 130 g) ball of mozzarella
2 tablespoons olive oil

For the crispy chicken, tip the flour into a wide bowl and add the garlic powder, onion powder, and paprika. Mix well and season with salt and pepper. Set aside.

In another wide bowl, whisk the eggs. Add the breadcrumbs, thyme, and half of the Parmesan to a third wide bowl and mix to combine. Set aside.

Using a sharp knife, slice the thickest part of the chicken breasts, about ½-inch (1 cm), making sure not to go right through.

Preheat the oven to 325°F (160°C).

Place a large sheet of wax paper on a clean counter. Using a rolling pin or meat hammer, bash one chicken breast evenly all over so it is the same thickness throughout, ideally, ½ inch (1 cm) thick. Continue with the other breast.

Place a large skillet over medium heat and add enough vegetable oil to cover the bottom of the skillet by ¾ inch (2 cm).

Working with one chicken breast at a time, dip it into the flour, tossing it around until evenly coated. Tap off any excess flour, then dip it into the egg, followed by the breadcrumbs, pressing it down to ensure an even coating. Sprinkle over half the remaining Parmesan and set aside. Do the same with the other chicken breast.

Once the oil is hot, fry one chicken breast at a time for 3 minutes on each side until deeply golden and crisp. Carefully remove with tongs and place on a baking sheet in the oven to keep warm while continuing with the other breast.

Meanwhile, for the salad, mix the nectarines, olives, cherry tomatoes, onion, lemon zest and juice, and parsley in a salad bowl. Top with the mozzarella and olive oil.

Serve the chicken with the salad.

Baked cod with lemon, cannellini beans, and a dill and pickle sauce

Serves: 2
Prep time: 10 minutes
Cook time: 30 to 40 minutes

This recipe is very simple as everything is cooked in a baking dish. Served with a delicious spicy aioli and a buttery white wine, it always impresses. Try to buy the jarred beans as they are cooked in a good stock, but if you only have canned beans, then just drain and add 1⅔ cups (400 ml) of vegetable stock instead.

4¾ cups (700 g) jarred cannellini beans in stock
¾ cup (180 ml) white wine
1 preserved lemon, thinly sliced and pips removed
3 shallots, quartered
3 garlic cloves, sliced
1 head of fennel, diced
2 (6-ounce / 170 g) cod filets, skinned and deboned
1 lemon, thinly sliced into rounds
1 handful of pitted green olives
3 tablespoons olive oil
Salt and pepper
1 handful of dill, for garnish

FOR THE PICKLE SAUCE
1 small bunch of dill, finely chopped
Scant ½ cup (100 g) mayonnaise
1 garlic clove, minced
1 large dill pickle, chopped
2 tablespoons pickle juice

Preheat the oven to 400°F (200°C).

Add the cannellini beans and their liquid to an 8 by 12 inches (20 by 30 cm) high-sided baking sheet. Pour in the wine.

Add the preserved lemon, then sprinkle with the shallots, garlic, and fennel. Top with the cod and season well with salt and pepper.

Place the lemon slices around the fish and sprinkle over the olives. Drizzle with the olive oil and bake in the oven for 20 minutes.

Meanwhile, for the dill sauce, mix the dill, mayonnaise, and garlic together in a bowl. Add the pickle with the pickle juice. Season with a pinch of salt, then taste and add more juice, if you like it spicy.

Once the fish is just flaky and cooked perfectly, ladle the beans into a bowl, then top with the fish and good dollop of the pickle sauce. Garnish with dill and serve.

DATE NIGHTS 105

Pistachio and ricotta gnudi with butter and sage sauce

Serves: 2
Prep Time: 10 minutes
Cook Time: 20 minutes

3½ tablespoons extra-virgin olive oil
2 garlic cloves
2 ounces (60 g) spinach
1 red chile, finely chopped
¾ cup (180 g) strained ricotta
Zest of 1 lemon
¼ cup (30 g) chopped toasted pistachios
½ cup (70 g) spelt flour, plus extra for dusting
1 handful of grated Parmesan, for sprinkling
Salt and pepper

FOR THE SAUCE
5 tablespoons (75 g) butter
1 bunch of sage, leaves picked

These lighter-than-air dumplings are made throughout Italy. I serve mine with a simple brown butter sauce and grated Parmesan. You can make these dumplings up to 6 hours in advance. Store in the refrigerator, then simply make the sauce and quickly cook them.

Heat the olive oil in a large skillet, add the garlic, and fry until crisp, 2 minutes. Add the spinach and chile and fry for another 2 minutes, or until the spinach has wilted.

Place the spinach mixture in a clean dish towel and squeeze out any excess liquid. Finely chop the mixture and add it to a large bowl.

Add the ricotta, lemon zest, nuts, flour, and a large pinch of salt and pepper to the bowl and mix gently until a dough comes together.

Half-fill a large saucepan with water and place over high heat. Lightly flour a large baking sheet. Roll the ricotta mixture into 10 small chestnut-size balls and add them to the baking sheet.

Once the water in the pan has reached a rolling boil, gently drop the dumplings in and cook until they all rise and bob to the surface, 3 to 4 minutes. Drain in a colander and set aside.

For the sauce, heat the butter in a medium skillet over medium heat until bubbling. Add the sage leaves and fry until the butter has turned golden and the sage is crisp, 2 minutes.

Toss in the gnudi, then remove the skillet from the heat. Divide the gnudi between two serving plates, then drizzle the brown butter and sage leaves all over, seasoning well with salt and pepper. Sprinkle with Parmesan and serve.

DATE NIGHTS 107

SOME SPECIAL

WEEKEND

THING FOR
FOR
THE

(and the magic of leftovers)

SOMETHING SPECIAL FOR THE WEEKEND

My perfect red wine ragù

Serves: 2
Prep Time: 20 minutes
Cook Time: 90 minutes

This ragù is perfect and often leaves enough leftovers to make my infamous lasagna on page 112. If you are not using the leftover ragù the next day, then simply freeze the remaining ragù in a freezerproof container.

Scant ½ cup (100 ml) olive oil
4 carrots, finely chopped
2 white onions, finely chopped
6 garlic cloves, finely chopped
4 celery stalks, diced
Juice of 1 lemon
3 rosemary sprigs, chopped
14 ounces (400 g) ground beef, 15% fat
14 ounces (400 g) ground pork, 15% fat
1 teaspoon fennel seeds
½ teaspoon red pepper flakes
1 teaspoon grated black pepper
2 cups (480 ml) red wine
3 (14-ounce / 400 g) cans plum tomatoes
1 teaspoon brown sugar
7 ounces (200 g) pappardelle or pasta of your choice
1 handful of basil leaves
Grated Parmesan
Olive oil, for drizzling
Kosher salt

Pour the olive oil into a wide, cast-iron pot with a lid. Add the carrots, onions, garlic, celery, and 2 teaspoons of salt and sweat the vegetables over medium heat for 15 minutes, stirring frequently. Add the lemon juice and cook for 5 minutes.

Using a slotted spoon, transfer the vegetables to a bowl, leaving the oil behind. Set aside.

Add the rosemary, beef, pork, fennel seeds, red pepper flakes, and black pepper to the pot and fry, stirring frequently until all the meat is browned, 6 minutes.

Pour in the wine and let the alcohol evaporate. Add the reserved vegetables, tomatoes, and sugar and stir, breaking the tomatoes up as you go. Bring to a bubble, cover with a lid, and simmer for 1 hour, stirring occasionally.

Uncover and cook until the sauce has reduced, is glossy and thick, 30 minutes.

Bring a large pan of water to a boil. Season with salt, add the pasta, and cook according to the package directions, or until al dente. Drain and add it back to the pan. Add as much ragù as you like and mix well. Ladle into bowls and top with basil, Parmesan, and a drizzle of olive oil.

LEFTOVER MAGIC...

DECADENT LASAGNA

Serves: 2
Prep Time: 5 minutes
Cook Time: 45 minutes

There is nothing like being served a perfect lasagna, oozing with melted cheese and a thick ragù sandwiched between layers of pasta. Serve with a simple bowl of arugula dressed with olive oil and balsamic vinegar and a glass of red wine. This recipe will make enough for now, and then you can refrigerate or freeze the leftover lasagna for another evening.

FOR THE WHITE SAUCE
2 tablespoons butter, ½ cup (60 g) all-purpose flour, 4¼ cups (1 L) milk of your choice, 1 cup (100 g) grated sharp cheddar, 1 teaspoon salt, ¼ teaspoon grated nutmeg

FOR THE LASAGNA
2½ cups (600 ml) leftover red wine ragu, 2 (5-ounce / 140 g) balls of mozzarella (drained), 1 bunch of basil leaves, 1 (9-ounce / 255 g) package dried lasagna sheets, ⅓ cup (30 g) grated Parmesan, olive oil (for drizzling)

Preheat the oven to 400°F (200°C).

For the white sauce, melt the butter in a heavy saucepan over medium heat. Add the flour and mix it together to form a paste, then fry for 2 minutes. Pour in the milk, a little at a time, whisking out any lumps as you go until all the milk is used up. Keep stirring until the sauce has thickened, 6 minutes.

Add the grated cheese, salt, and nutmeg and cook until the cheese has melted. Taste and add more salt if needed. Remove from the heat.

To assemble the lasagna, ladle one-third of the ragù into an 8 by 12-inch (20 by 30 cm) high-sided baking sheet and top with one-third of the white sauce. Tear over one-third of the mozzarella and top with a sprinkling of basil. Top with a layer of lasagna sheets, then repeat two times finishing with a layer of white sauce.

Top with the remaining mozzarella and all the grated Parmesan, then drizzle with a little olive oil. Bake in the oven until bubbling and golden brown on top, 25 minutes.

Let cool for 10 minutes before serving.

SOMETHING SPECIAL FOR THE WEEKEND

One-pan roast chicken with lemon and herb butter and roasted shallots

Serves: 2
Prep Time: 10 minutes
Cook Time: 75 minutes

1 (4¼-pound / 2 kg) whole chicken
7 tablespoons (100 g) softened butter
1 small bunch of tarragon, chopped
1 small bunch of parsley, chopped
1 head of garlic, halved and 3 garlic cloves, grated, divided
2 lemons, grated zest of 1 and both sliced, divided
10 banana shallots, halved
10 small new potatoes
1 tablespoon olive oil
2 cups (480 ml) white wine
1 tablespoon Dijon mustard
Kosher salt

FOR THE STOCK

1¼ pounds (570 g) any leftover vegetable in the refrigerator. I had 2 onions, 3 carrots, a celery stalk, and 1 leek
9 cups (2.2 L) water

Here, I show you how to make the most succulent roast chicken ever. Once you have eaten the chicken, make a stock with the leftovers and you have two meals out of one bird. If you are not planning to make the Chicken Tortellini on page 116 in the next couple of days, simply freeze the cooked chicken and stock, then defrost before making it.

Preheat the oven to 475°F (250°C). Remove the chicken from the refrigerator and set aside.

Add the butter, herbs, grated garlic, and lemon zest to a bowl. Season well with salt and mix.

Carefully push your fingers between the skin and breast meat of the chicken to create a pocket. Spoon three-quarters of the herb butter under the skin and spread it out evenly. Smear the remaining butter over the outside of the chicken.

Add the shallots and potatoes to an 8 by 12-inch (20 by 30 cm) high-sided baking sheet. Add the halved garlic and sliced lemons. Pour over the olive oil and season with salt. Place the chicken on top and pour in the wine. Season the chicken skin generously with salt. Roast with the legs facing the back of the oven for 25 minutes. Reduce the heat to 350°F (180°C) and roast for another 45 minutes.

When the chicken is cooked, let it rest on a platter for 15 minutes. Add the mustard to the baking sheet and mix well. Return the sheet with the vegetables to the oven for 10 minutes.

Carve the bird. Ladle enough of the vegetables and sauce from the baking sheet into bowls, making sure to pull out five potatoes each. Top with the sliced chicken, and serve with a crisp salad, if desired.

For the stock, add the remaining vegetables for the stock to a stockpot. Set aside any leftover shallots from the baking sheet. Tear all the meat off the chicken and set it aside with the shallots.

Add the bones to the pot. Pour in the water and add all the juices from the baking sheet, scraping any bits into the pot. Bring to a boil and simmer for 1 to 2 hours.

Strain the stock, pushing all the liquid out of the strainer as you go. Chill in the refrigerator for a few days or freeze until needed.

SOMETHING SPECIAL FOR THE WEEKEND

LEFTOVER MAGIC...

ROAST CHICKEN AND RICOTTA TORTELLINI IN BROTH

Serves: 2
Prep Time: 40 minutes
Cook Time: 6 minutes

For me, there is nothing more satisfying than making fresh pasta. It always feels like an act of love. I like to do this on a Sunday when the day feels long and slow. This is ideal after making the roast chicken as really only a few more ingredients are needed.

FOR THE PASTA
1¾ cups (200 g) type "00" pasta flour (plus extra for dusting), 2 large eggs

FOR THE FILLING
3½ ounces (100 g) leftover roast chicken (diced), 2 leftover roast shallots (diced), scant ½ cup (100 g) fresh ricotta, 1 red chile (diced), zest of 1 lemon, 1 tablespoon chopped basil, 1 tablespoon grated Parmesan, salt and pepper

FOR SERVING
3 cups (720 ml) chicken stock (either from page 114 or store-bought), ¾ cup (100 g) fresh or frozen peas, 1 handful of basil leaves, ¼ cup (20 g) grated Parmesan, olive oil (for drizzling)

For the pasta dough, mix the flour and eggs in a food processor until it forms a ball of dough. Tip it out onto a clean counter and knead until you have a smooth and silky dough, 5 minutes. Cover the dough with plastic wrap and rest in the refrigerator for 30 minutes.

Meanwhile, for the filling, add the chicken and shallots to a large bowl. Add the ricotta, chile, lemon zest, basil, and Parmesan. Season to taste with salt, and add a good pinch of pepper.

Remove the rested dough from the refrigerator and cut in half. Working with one-half at a time and keeping the other covered, use a pasta machine to roll the dough out. Start with the widest setting, then go up to the thinnest until you have a long, thin sheet of pasta.

Lay the pasta sheet out on a clean counter, and stamp out 15 rounds using a fluted 3¼-inch (8 cm) cookie cutter. Continue with the rest of the dough.

Lightly flour a baking sheet. Place 1 small teaspoon of the filling into the center of one of the rounds, then fold one side over toward you, creating a half-moon, and seal the edges with your fingers. Fold the half-moon back over, giving you a crown, and bring the sides round. Pinch the sides to make a tortellini shape. Continue with the remaining pasta, placing them on the sheet.

Bring the stock to a boil in a pan and bring a pot half-full of water to a boil. Season the pot well with salt, add the pasta, and cook until they have floated to the surface, 1 to 2 minutes. Drain and scoop into serving bowls.

Add the peas to the broth, then remove from the heat. Ladle into the bowls and top with the basil, Parmesan, and olive oil.

SOMETHING SPECIAL FOR THE WEEKEND

SOMETHING SPECIAL FOR THE WEEKEND

My carnitas tacos

Serves: 2
Prep Time: 10 minutes
Cook Time: 2 hours

Traveling to Mexico blew my mind with its magical beaches, towns, beautiful people, and unbelievably delicious food. I serve these tacos with a spicy green salsa, diced onion, and lime wedges. Personally, I think you need nothing more, except for an ice-cold Pacifico, but that's up to you.

FOR THE PORK
3 tablespoons lard
Juice of 1 orange
Juice of 1 lime
1 white onion, coarsely chopped
4 garlic cloves, bashed
1 cinnamon stick
3 jalapeños
1 brined poblano pepper
2¼ pounds (1 kg) pork shoulder, cut into 2-inch (5 cm) pieces
1 (12-ounce / 360 ml) bottle of Mexican beer

FOR THE GREEN SALSA
2 jalapeños
5 tomatillos, husked and rinsed
1 garlic clove, peeled
⅛ bunch of cilantro
1 teaspoon salt
Juice of 1 lime

FOR SERVING
8 corn tortillas, warmed
1 white onion, diced
1 lime, cut into wedges
1 handful of cilantro

Add the lard to a wide heavy, pan with a lid, and place over high heat. Add the orange and lime juices, onion, garlic, and cinnamon. Add the chiles, top with the pork, and fry, stirring frequently, for another 10 minutes.

Pour in the beer, then reduce the heat to medium and bring to a simmer. Reduce the heat to low, cover with the lid, and cook for 90 minutes, stirring occasionally.

Meanwhile, for the green salsa, blitz the chiles, tomatillos, garlic, cilantro, salt, and lime juice in a food processor until it is a chunky green consistency. Taste and add a little more salt if needed. Transfer to a bowl and set aside.

After 90 minutes, remove the lid from the pork and cook until the liquid has reduced and thickened and the pork is falling apart, 30 minutes. Take the pan off the heat and remove most of the pork fat, leaving behind 3½ ounces (100 g). Shred the pork and chiles in the pan.

Serve the pork with tortillas, diced onion, lime wedges, cilantro, and the salsa.

LEFTOVER MAGIC...

Serves: 2
Prep Time: 5 minutes
Cook Time: 30 minutes

SPICY BLACK BEAN STEW

2 tablespoons lard or olive oil, 1 red onion (diced), 3 garlic cloves (sliced), 2 poblano chiles (sliced), 1 small bunch of Mexican thyme leaves, 1 teaspoon sweet paprika, 1 teaspoon ground coriander, ½ teaspoon ground cumin, 1 tablespoon chipotle chili paste, 1 (14-ounce / 400 g) can chopped tomatoes, 9 ounces (255 g) leftover pork carnitas, 2 cups (510 g) jarred black beans, juice of 2 limes, salt

FOR SERVING
1 avocado (sliced), 8 pickled jalapeños, 2 tablespoons sour cream, 1 handful of cilantro leaves, lime wedges

Add the lard to a large, heavy saucepan and place over medium heat. Add the onion and fry for 5 minutes. Add the garlic and chiles and fry for a few more minutes. Add the thyme, paprika, coriander, cumin, and chipotle paste and fry, stirring frequently, for another 2 minutes.

Add the chopped tomatoes, leftover pork, beans, and the liquid they are in. Season with salt and cook until reduced and thickened, 20 minutes.

Add the lime juice, then taste and add more salt if needed. If at this point the stew is too thick, add a little boiling water.

Ladle the stew into bowls and top with sliced avocado, pickled jalapeños, a dollop of sour cream, cilantro leaves, and lime wedges.

Spicy makhani paneer curry and parathas

Serves: 2
Prep Time: 10 minutes
Cook Time: 25 to 30 minutes

This decadent curry is perfectly paired with my easy-to-make flaky parathas. Don't be fearful of the shopping list; it's mainly spices, which you hopefully have in the pantry already. If you are serving this as a feast, accompany it with a chopped cucumber, tomato, and red onion salad.

1½-inch (4 cm) piece of ginger, peeled
2 garlic cloves, peeled
1 Indian green chile
2 tablespoons Greek yogurt
2 teaspoons gram (chickpea) flour
1 teaspoon chili powder
¼ teaspoon garam masala
1 teaspoon ground coriander
14 ounces (400 g) paneer, cut into bite-size cubes

FOR THE SAUCE

2 tablespoons salted butter
2 onions, thinly sliced
5 green cardamom pods lightly crushed
1 cinnamon stick
1½-inch (4 cm) piece of ginger, peeled and grated
2 green Indian chiles, cut lengthwise
2 teaspoons Kashmiri chile powder
¼ teaspoon garam masala
3 tablespoons tomato paste
¾ cup (180 ml) heavy cream
1 teaspoon brown sugar
⅔ cup (160 ml) water
1 large handful of cilantro, chopped

FOR THE PARATHA

1 (11-ounce / 320 g) puff pastry sheet
All-purpose flour, for dusting and coating

Blend the ginger, garlic, and chile in a blender until smooth. In a bowl, combine the yogurt and flour. Add the ginger paste, chili powder, garam masala, coriander, and paneer and mix until the paneer is coated in the marinade. Let stand.

For the sauce, heat the butter in a saucepan over medium heat. Add the onions and sauté until they are soft and sticky, 10 to 15 minutes. Add the cardamom and cinnamon and fry for another 2 minutes. Add the ginger and chiles and fry for 1 minute. Add the chile powder, garam masala, and tomato paste and cook for 2 minutes, stirring frequently. Gradually stir in the cream and sugar. Pour in the water, then reduce the heat to low and simmer while you cook the paneer.

Preheat the broiler to medium. Thread the marinated paneer onto four metal skewers and place them on a baking sheet. Broil for 10 minutes on each side until golden and charred.

For the paratha, roll the pastry on a floured counter into a sausage and slice it into four pieces. Squash the pieces between your palms to form a patty. Coat both sides of the patty with flour, then roll it out into a 7 to 8-inch (18 to 20 cm) round. Repeat with the remaining pastry.

Heat a skillet over medium to high heat. Fry a paratha for 1 minute on each side. Remove and repeat with the other parathas.

Pull the paneer off the skewers into the sauce and add the cilantro. Serve with the parathas.

SOMETHING SPECIAL FOR THE WEEKEND

LEFTOVER MAGIC...

Serves: 2
Prep Time: 10 minutes
Cook Time: 40 minutes

BAKED RICE AND HERB SALAD

If you have never baked rice before, this is a great place to start. Using my delicious leftover curry gives you a depth of flavor with zero effort.

15 cherry tomatoes, 1 red onion (sliced), 2 tablespoons ghee, 1 cinnamon stick, 1 bunch of cilantro (sliced), 1½ cups (350 g) leftover makhani curry, ¾ cup (150 g) basmati rice, 2 tablespoons boiling water, juice of ½ lemon, kosher salt

FOR THE SALAD
juice of ½ lemon, 1 tablespoon mango chutney, 2 tablespoons olive oil, 1 garlic clove (grated), 1 Indian red chile (sliced), ½ cucumber, 1 carrot, 1 handful of mint, 1 handful of cilantro, 1 red onion (sliced), salt

Preheat the oven to 400°F (200°C).

Add the tomatoes, onion, ghee, cinnamon, and cilantro to an 8 by 12-inch (20 by 30 cm) baking dish and roast for 20 minutes.

Add the leftover curry and mix together. Spread the rice on top and season with salt. Carefully pour over the boiling water, cover with foil, and roast for 20 minutes.

For the salad, mix the lemon juice, chutney, olive oil, garlic, and chile in a bowl until well combined. Season to taste with salt. Using a vegetable peeler, peel long strips of cucumber and carrot into the bowl. Add the herbs and onion and mix.

When the rice is ready, remove from the oven and leave, covered, for 10 minutes. Uncover and add the lemon juice. Serve with the salad.

SOMETHING SPECIAL FOR THE WEEKEND

Spicy crispy gyoza with smashed cucumber salad

Makes: 30 dumplings
Prep Time: 10 minutes
Cook Time: 40 minutes

These crispy, succulent dumplings are so much better than store-bought ones. They freeze really well or can be kept in the refrigerator for a few days. Serve with a zingy bashed cucumber salad and some spicy Sriracha sauce, if desired.

FOR THE DUMPLINGS
1½-inch (4 cm) piece of ginger, peeled and grated
2 garlic cloves, grated
2 red chiles, finely diced
2 scallions, finely chopped
9 ounces (250 g) ground pork
2 tablespoons Shaoxing wine
1 tablespoon light soy sauce
1 teaspoon sesame oil
24 dumpling wrappers
2 tablespoons peanut oil
⅔ cup (160 ml) water, divided
2 tablespoons cornstarch
Toasted sesame seeds, for garnish
Sriracha sauce, for serving

FOR THE SALAD
1 cucumber, halved, bashed with the back of a knife, and diagonally sliced
1 garlic clove, grated
2 tablespoons rice vinegar
2 tablespoons soy sauce
2 tablespoons crispy chili oil (I used Lee Kum Kee)
2 teaspoons sesame oil
1½ teaspoons sugar

For the dumplings, add the garlic, ginger, chile, most of the scallions, and the pork to a large bowl. Using clean hands, squish all the ingredients together until they are well combined. Add the wine, soy sauce, and sesame oil and mix until combined.

Place one of the wrappers into the palm of your hand. Keep the rest of the wrappers covered with a damp paper towel. Spoon an olive-size amount of the filling into the middle of the wrapper. Use your finger to dampen the edge of the wrapper with a little water. Fold the wrapper in half, pleat the edge, and press down to seal. Repeat until you've used up all the filling. The dumplings can be stored in the refrigerator for two days or in the freezer for a few months.

Place a large skillet with a lid over medium heat. Add the peanut oil and arrange 12 dumplings around the pan in a circular shape. Fry until the bottoms of the dumplings are golden brown and crisp, 6 minutes. Pour in scant ½ cup (100 ml) water, cover with a lid, and cook for 3 minutes.

Meanwhile, for the cucumber salad, mix the cucumber slices, garlic, vinegar, soy sauce, oils, and sugar together in a bowl.

Mix the cornstarch with the ¼ cup (60 ml) water and pour it over the dumplings. Cover with a lid and fry until the cornstarch has created a lacy crisp layer, 6 minutes. Flip onto a plate and sprinkle with the remaining scallions and the sesame seeds. Serve with the salad and Sriracha.

LEFTOVER MAGIC...

GYOZA IN BROTH WITH CHILI CRISP AND GREENS

Serves: 2
Prep Time: 10 minutes
Cook Time: 15 minutes

A steamy bowl of miso broth with homemade dumplings is always comforting on those chilly evenings. Make the gyoza in advance, then all you need to do is to prepare the broth.

2 tablespoons peanut oil, 1½-inch (4 cm) piece of ginger (peeled and julienned), 2 garlic cloves (sliced), 1 red chile (sliced on the bias), 12 gyoza (see page 125), 2 scallions (white parts sliced into ½-inch / 1 cm rounds; green parts thinly sliced and used for garnish), 3 cups (720 ml) chicken stock, 1 tablespoon white miso paste, 1 tablespoon Shaoxing rice wine vinegar, 1 tablespoon soy sauce, 2 cups (100 g) spinach, 2 tablespoons chili crisp oil

In a wide saucepan large enough to hold the gyoza and broth, add the oil and place over medium heat. Add the ginger, garlic, and chile and fry for a few minutes until the garlic is crisp and golden. Remove with a slotted spoon and set aside.

Add the gyoza to the pan and fry until the bottoms are golden and crisp, 6 minutes. Add the white part of the scallions and fry for 1 minute.

Pour in the stock and whisk in the miso until everything is combined. Add the vinegar and soy sauce and simmer for another 6 minutes.

Add the spinach and the reserved fried garlic, ginger, and chile and cook until the spinach has wilted, 2 minutes. Ladle into bowls, drizzle over the chili crisp and garnish with the remaining scallions.

SOMETHING SPECIAL FOR THE WEEKEND

Crispy pork belly with fennel and potato gratin

Serves: 2
Prep Time: 10 minutes
Cook Time: 120 minutes

This crispy pork belly dish and the accompanying decadent fennel and potato gratin are perfect served with simple steamed lemony greens. The pork drippings and roasted apples make a delicious gravy, perfect for drizzling over everything.

1 (2¼ pounds / 1 kg) pork belly
1 teaspoon fennel seeds
2 tablespoons sea salt
3 apples, cut into 6 wedges
2 red onions
Olive oil, for drizzling
1 (17-ounce / 500 ml) bottle of cloudy cider
1 tablespoon butter
5 ounces (140 g) Tuscan kale, for serving
Juice of ½ lemon, for serving

FOR THE FENNEL GRATIN

14 ounces (400 g) russet potatoes, peeled and very thinly sliced
2 heads of fennel, very thinly sliced
3 garlic cloves, grated
¾ cup (180 ml) heavy cream
Scant ½ cup (100 ml) half and half
1 tablespoon Dijon mustard
¾ cup (100 g) grated Gruyère cheese
1 small bunch of sage
Salt and pepper

Using a sharp knife, make six slits into the pork fat about ¼-inch (5 mm) thick. Bash the fennel seeds in a mortar and pestle, add the salt, and mix until combined. Rub the fennel salt all over the skin. You can do this the day before and leave it uncovered in the refrigerator.

When ready to cook, preheat the oven to 400°C (200°C). Add the apples and onions to a large baking sheet. Drizzle with a little oil, then lay the pork on top and roast for 40 minutes.

For the gratin, add the potatoes and fennel to a bowl with the garlic and both creams. Mix in the mustard and season very well. Tip half the potato mix into an 8 by 12-inch (20 by 30 cm) small baking dish and sprinkle with half the cheese. Add a layer of sage, then tip in the remaining potato mix. Press it down and finish with a layer of sage and the remaining cheese.

After 30 minutes, remove the pork and carefully pour in the cider. Reduce the oven temperature to 325°F (160°C) and roast for 1 hour. Bake the gratin on the same shelf if possible.

When the pork is cooked, remove both dishes from the oven and transfer the pork to a platter. Using a masher, mash all the ingredients on the sheet together. Pour the gravy through a strainer into a small pan. Place over high heat and add the butter. Cook until reduced, 6 minutes.

Steam the greens, then dress with lemon juice, salt, and olive oil. Slice the pork and serve with the gratin, greens, and gravy.

SOMETHING SPECIAL FOR THE WEEKEND

LEFTOVER MAGIC...

CRISPY PORK BANH MI

Serves: 2
Prep Time: 15 minutes
Cook Time: 10 minutes

After you have made the most delicious and decadent roast pork and fennel and potato gratin (see page 128), you may want something spicy to mix things up. My quick banh mi is a take on a Vietnamese sandwich and is perfect for a big lunch or dinner. If you can't find Vietnamese baguettes, then any white fluffy baguette will do.

FOR THE SANDWICH
7 ounces (200 g) roast pork belly (sliced), 2 long, crusty Vietnamese baguettes, 4 tablespoons chicken liver or pork pâte, 2 tablespoons mayonnaise, 4 long strips of cucumber, 1 handful of cilantro, 1 red chile (sliced diagonally), 2 teaspoons Maggi seasoning or soy sauce, 1 large squeeze of Sriracha sauce (for serving, optional)

FOR THE PICKLED CARROT
¾ cup (180 ml) hot water, ¼ cup (50 g) superfine sugar, 2 teaspoons salt, ⅔ cup (160 ml) rice wine vinegar, 2 carrots (cut into very thin matchsticks)

Preheat the oven to 350°F (180°C).

Place the pork slices on a baking sheet and heat in the oven to get crisp.

For the carrots, pour the hot water into a heatproof bowl. Add the sugar and salt and mix until dissolved. Pour in the vinegar, add the carrots, and let chill in the refrigerator for 20 minutes or up to a week.

If the baguettes aren't very crispy, pop them in the oven for a few minutes. Slice the baguettes down the middle but keep the bread intact down one side. Spread the pâte evenly across the baguettes and top with the mayonnaise.

Drain the carrots and pile onto each baguette. Once the pork is warmed through, top with equal slices of pork. Place long strips of cucumber on top followed by a good amount of cilantro and chile. Finish with a couple splashes of seasoning on each and eat immediately with a squeeze of Sriracha, if you like it spicy.

SOMETHING SPECIAL FOR THE WEEKEND

MOMENTS

SWEET

FOR

TWO

My heavenly Calvados tiramisu

Serves: 2
Prep Time: 20 minutes

Tiramisu is extremely simple to whip up. When making for two, I like to make it just before serving so the ladyfingers are still crunchy. Calvados is a French brandy made from apples, but if you can't find it, then use vin santo, an Italian dessert wine made from grapes, instead.

1 cup (240 ml) good hot coffee
2 tablespoons Calvados
1 large egg, separated
¼ cup (50 g) superfine sugar
¾ cup (180 g) mascarpone
3½ tablespoons heavy cream
1 teaspoon vanilla bean paste
8 ladyfingers
1 tablespoon unsweetened cocoa powder
¼ cup (20 g) grated semisweet (dark) chocolate

Pour the coffee into a heatproof bowl with the Calvados and let cool for 10 minutes.

Using an electric hand whisk, whisk the egg white in a large bowl until almost stiff peaks form. Add the sugar and continue to whisk until lightly glossy.

Whisk the egg yolk in another large bowl until pale and fluffy. Add the mascarpone, cream, and vanilla and lightly whisk together. Gently fold the egg white into the cream until fully mixed.

Dunk the ladyfingers one at a time for a few seconds into the cooled coffee mix, then lay two in the bottom of each bowl or glass. Top with a generous dollop of cream, then repeat with another layer. Finish with the remaining cream, a dusting of cocoa, and some grated chocolate.

SWEET MOMENTS FOR TWO

136 SWEET MOMENTS FOR TWO

Plum upside-down cake with lemon zest

Serves: 2
Prep Time: 5 minutes
Cook Time: 40 minutes

This is one of those recipes that is very adaptable. I make it into a tray bake or muffins or use whatever fruit is in season at the time. In summer, I use nectarines and cherries; in the fall, I love plums or pears; in winter I will use local apples; and in spring, it is delicious made with apricots.

⅞ cup plus 6 tablespoons (200 g) unsalted butter, softened, plus extra for greasing
3 tablespoons soft light brown sugar
10 ounces (280 g) plums, pitted and halved or quartered
½ cup plus 1 tablespoon (110 g) superfine sugar
2 eggs
1 teaspoon vanilla bean paste
Zest of 1 unwaxed lemon
1 cup plus 2 tablespoons (150 g) self-rising flour
1 teaspoon baking powder
1 pinch of salt
1 tablespoon milk
Heavy cream, for serving

Preheat the oven to 350°F (180°C). Grease the sides of a 6-inch (15 cm) cake pan with butter and line the bottom with wax paper.

Add the brown sugar and ¼ cup (60 g) of the butter to a small skillet and melt over medium heat. Once melted, pour into the prepared pan, then arrange the fruit cut-side down in the pan.

Whisk the remaining butter and the superfine sugar in a stand mixer fitted with a whisk attachment until pale and light in texture. Gradually add an egg, mixing for a minute or so before you add the next. Add the vanilla and lemon zest.

Sift the flour, baking powder, and salt into the bowl, then add the milk and fold together until smooth. Carefully spoon the batter over the fruit, using the back of a spoon to flatten it out.

Bake for 40 minutes, or until risen, golden brown, and a skewer inserted into the middle of the cake comes out clean.

Let the cake cool in the pan for 1 minute, then carefully turn it out onto a serving plate. Remove the wax paper and let cool slightly before serving with plenty of heavy cream. This cake is best served warm.

138 SWEET MOMENTS FOR TWO

Warm brown butter cookie cake with ice cream

Serves: 2
Prep Time: 2 minutes
Cook Time: 15 minutes

The thing I crave the most when I need sugar is a fresh baked cookie; it hits the spot always and this one is perfect when you have basic staples in the pantry. You can use any nuts you love. This can be made and frozen for those times when you need a sugar kick quick. I always double the recipe and make one for now, one for later.

- ¼ cup (60 g) salted butter
- ¼ cup plus 2½ tablespoons (80 g) light brown sugar
- 2 tablespoons granulated sugar
- 1 egg, whisked
- 2 teaspoons vanilla bean paste
- ¾ cup (100 g) all-purpose flour
- ½ teaspoon baking soda
- 1 large pinch of flaky sea salt
- ⅓ cup (50 g) chopped semisweet (dark) chocolate
- ⅓ cup (40 g) chopped macadamia nuts
- 3 scoops of vanilla ice cream

Preheat the oven to 400°F (200°C).

Heat the butter in a small ovenproof 7½-inch (19 cm) skillet over medium heat, swirling the mixture around until the butter turns a golden brown color and making sure not to burn the butter. Remove from the heat and pour into the bowl of a stand mixer fitted with a whisk attachment. Let cool.

Once the butter has cooled, add both sugars and whisk until smooth. Add the egg and vanilla bean paste to the butter mix and whisk until smooth, 3 minutes.

Fold in the flour, baking soda, salt, chocolate, and nuts. Pour the batter into the skillet you used to melt the butter, then transfer to the oven and bake for 12 minutes.

Remove the skillet from the oven and let stand for 5 minutes. Serve warm with ice cream.

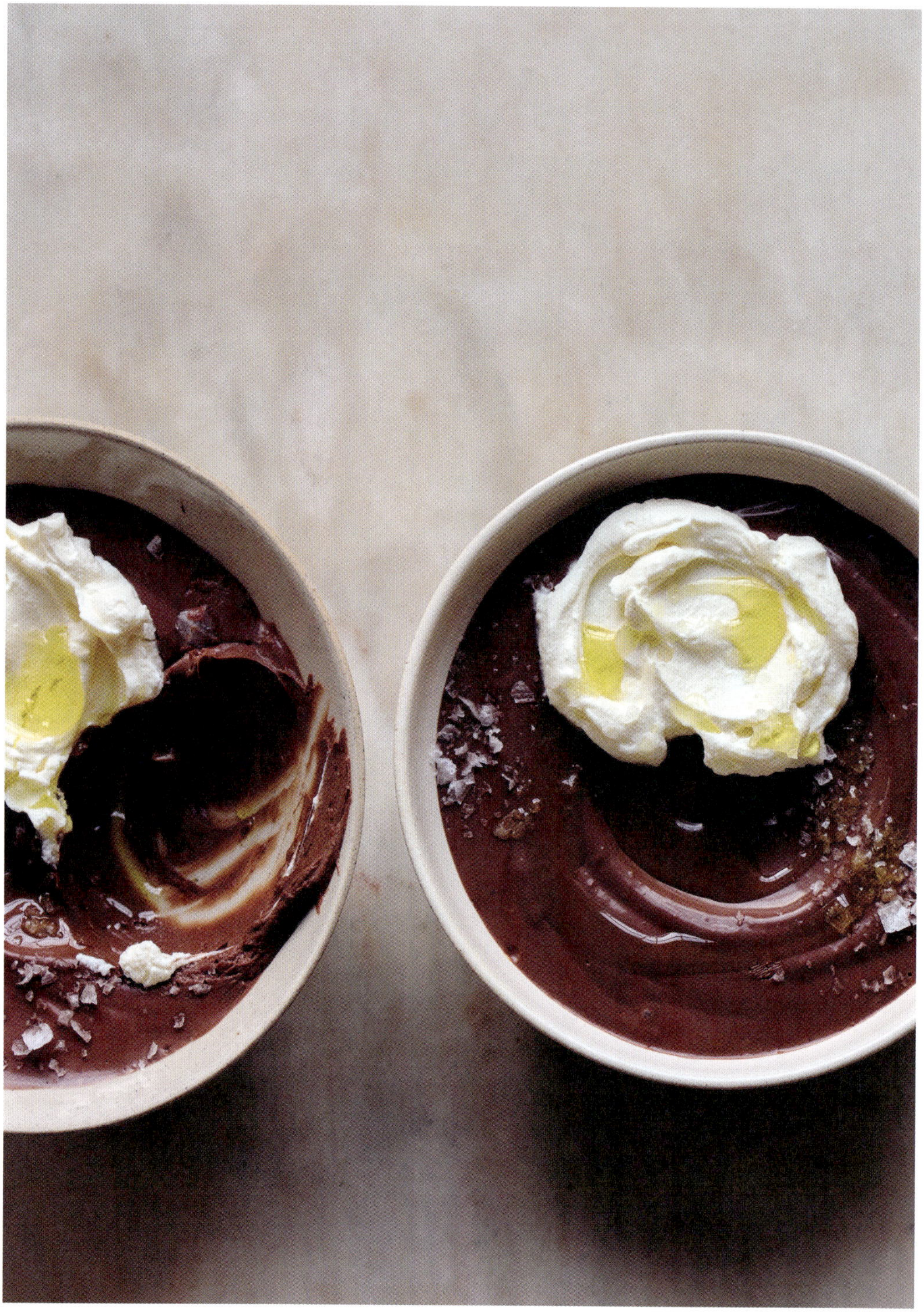

Earl Grey chocolate pudding

Serves 2
Prep Time: 15 minutes + chilling
Cook Time: 10 minutes

These velvety chocolate mousse puddings are light and rich at the same time. You can make them a day ahead and store them in the refrigerator overnight.

Scant ½ cup (100 ml) boiling water
Zest of 1 orange
Scant ½ cup (100 ml) maple syrup
1 teaspoon vanilla bean paste
1 Earl Grey tea bag
2 tablespoons unsweetened cocoa powder
3½ ounces (100 g) semisweet (dark) chocolate (at least 70% cocoa solids), broken into pieces
1 (10-ounce / 280 g) block of silken tofu
2 tablespoons crème fraîche
1 tablespoon olive oil
Sea salt

Pour the boiling water into a heatproof bowl, add the orange zest, maple syrup, vanilla bean paste, and tea bag, and let stand for 5 minutes. Remove the tea bag and whisk in the cocoa.

Melt the chocolate in another heatproof bowl set over a small pan of boiling water, making sure the bottom of the bowl isn't touching the water.

Add the tofu to a clean dish towel and squeeze out the excess water. Tip the tofu into a food processor and blend until very smooth.

With the food processor still running, pour in the chocolate, followed by the tea mix.

Spoon into two bowls and chill in the refrigerator for 1 hour, or overnight. Top with a dollop of crème fraîche, a drizzle of olive oil, and a good sprinkling of sea salt.

Banana, rum, and lime tarte tatin

Serves: 2
Prep Time: 5 minutes
Cook Time: 25 minutes

This rum and caramelized banana tarte tatin is the perfect finish for any meal. The crisp flaky pastry holds the caramelized bananas and rum caramel together perfectly. I love to serve this tart with a coconut gelato, but vanilla ice cream is great, too.

1 (11-ounce / 320 g) all-butter puff pastry sheet
½ cup (100 g) superfine sugar
¼ cup (60 ml) rum
Zest of 1 lime
2 tablespoons butter
½ teaspoon ground cinnamon
Sea salt
3 medium ripe bananas, peeled and sliced into 1½-inch (4 cm) chunks
2 scoops of coconut gelato, for serving

Preheat the oven to 400°F (200°C).

Place the pastry sheet over a medium, ovenproof skillet and cut out a slightly larger circle than the pan. Transfer the pastry round to the refrigerator and chill until needed.

Add the sugar to the skillet and place over medium heat. You want all the sugar to dissolve and caramelize so be careful. Tip the pan every now and again making sure the sugar is melting evenly. After the sugar has become a golden caramel, carefully pour in the rum and lime zest, then leave on the heat for 1 minute.

Whisk the butter into the caramel, then add the cinnamon and a good pinch of salt.

Arrange the bananas in a single layer in the caramel, then cover the bananas with the chilled pastry. Using a butter knife, tuck in the edges. Cut a small cross in the center of the pastry to allow steam to escape and bake until golden brown and crisp, 15 to 20 minutes. Let the tart cool for 5 minutes in the skillet, then carefully flip upside down onto a plate and serve with gelato.

SWEET MOMENTS FOR TWO

Orange blossom and lemon granita

Serves 2
Prep Time: 10 minutes + freezing
Cook Time: 5 minutes

This is the most refreshing, almost sherbety granita ever. I always make extra, and keep any leftovers in the freezer. On those hot evenings, I pour some tequila over the top for a speedy cocktail and for a kitsch serve, I freeze a couple of hollowed-out lemons, then serve the granita in them.

⅓ cup (35 g) cornstarch
1⅔ cups (400 ml) water
½ cup (100 g) superfine sugar
4 lemons, 2 zested and juice of 2 lemons
Juice of 1 orange
1 tablespoon orange blossom water
1 handful of finely chopped pistachios

In a large saucepan, whisk the cornstarch and scant ½ cup (100 ml) water together until smooth. Pour in another 1¼ cups (300 ml) water, then add the sugar and place over medium heat. Keep stirring until the mixture thickens slightly and goes glossy.

Remove the pan from the heat. Add the lemon zest and citrus juice, then stir in the orange blossom water.

Pour the mixture into a freezerproof container and freeze for 12–24 hours until ice crystals form, removing it from the freezer every hour or so, and use a fork to break up any large ice crystals.

When ready to eat, simply fork into frozen lemons or bowls and top with a sprinkle of chopped pistachios.

SWEET MOMENTS FOR TWO

Miso and dark chocolate freezer cookies

If these cookies sound a bit out there for you, make them immediately! You will never know they had miso or soy in them. It just gives a deep umami flavor. They are baked until the outside is crisp but the inside is still soft and chewy.

Makes: 8
Prep Time: 2 minutes
Cook Time: 15 minutes

½ cup plus 1 tablespoon (110 g) unsalted butter
1¼ cups (165 g) all-purpose flour
½ teaspoon baking powder
¼ teaspoon baking soda
2 tablespoons white miso paste
1 teaspoon dark soy sauce
½ cup plus 2 tablespoons (120 g) granulated sugar
⅓ cup plus 1 teaspoon (70 g) dark brown sugar
1 large egg
1 teaspoon vanilla extract
¾ cup (100 g) chopped semisweet (dark) chocolate (at least 70% cocoa solids)
Sea salt, for sprinkling (optional)

Melt the butter in a small pan over medium heat, swirling the butter around until it turns a golden brown color and making sure not to burn it. Remove from the heat and pour into the bowl of a stand mixer fitted with a paddle attachment. Let cool.

In a medium bowl, sift the flour, baking powder, and baking soda and mix to combine.

Add the miso and soy sauce to the brown butter and beat on medium speed until combined. Add both the sugars and beat for another 2 minutes.

With the machine still running, add the egg and vanilla and mix vigorously until the mixture turns pale and creamy, 2 minutes.

Gently fold the dry ingredients into the egg mixture with a spoon, then fold in the chocolate.

Form the dough into 8 equal-size balls. If you have an ice cream or cookie scoop then use that.

You can either freeze the balls now for cooking later, or chill them in the refrigerator for 1 hour.

Preheat the oven to 350°F (180°C).

Arrange the cookies on a large baking sheet and bake for 13 minutes, or 15 minutes if cooking from frozen. Remove from the oven and let cool for 5 minutes on the baking sheet, then transfer to a cooling rack and let cool for another 20 minutes. Serve, sprinkled with sea salt, if desired.

Celebration chocolate Guinness cake

Serves 2
Prep Time: 10 minutes
Cook Time: 50 minutes

This cake is the one to make when you need a showstopper but don't want to make a huge cake. Guinness makes the texture of the cake very moist and fudge-like, so it always comes out perfectly and stores for a few days without drying out. For special occasions, I slice the cake in half, then use the frosting to sandwich the halves together, and pipe the rest of the frosting on the top, but for other times, I simply decorate the top of the cake with the frosting.

1⅛ sticks (125 g) salted butter, softened, plus extra for greasing
⅔ cup (160 ml) Guinness
¾ cup plus 2½ tablespoons (180 g) soft light brown sugar
⅓ cup (35 g) unsweetened cocoa powder
2 eggs
⅓ cup (80 g) sour cream
1 tablespoon vanilla extract
1 cup plus 1 tablespoon (140 g) all-purpose flour
1½ teaspoons baking soda
¼ cup (20 g) grated semisweet (dark) chocolate

FOR THE FROSTING
¾ cup (180 g) whole cream cheese
1 teaspoon vanilla bean paste
½ cup (70 g) confectioners' sugar
⅔ cup (160 ml) heavy cream

Preheat the oven to 350°F (180°C). Grease a 6¼-inch (16 cm) springform cake pan with butter and line the bottom with baking parchment.

Add the butter to a medium saucepan and pour in the Guinness. Place over low heat, stirring occasionally, until the butter has melted, then whisk in the brown sugar and cocoa. Remove the pan from the heat.

Whisk the eggs, sour cream, and vanilla in a large bowl until smooth. Add the Guinness mix and stir until combined. Add the flour and baking soda and mix well.

Pour the batter into the prepared pan and bake for 45 minutes until a crust has formed and it is still fudgy. Remove and let cool in the pan.

Once the cake is cold, make the frosting. Whisk the cream cheese, vanilla, confectioners' sugar, and cream in a large bowl until smooth and glossy yet holding its form.

Slice the cooled sponge in half. Spoon half the frosting in the middle and sandwich with the remaining cake. Decorate the top with the rest of the frosting. Sprinkle with chocolate.

SWEET MOMENTS FOR TWO

SWEET MOMENTS FOR TWO

Grated frozen nectarine with olive oil and salt over ice cream

This recipe is extremely simple, so when baking isn't on the plan for your evening, this will truly impress your guest. Make sure to use good-quality ice cream and extra-virgin olive oil.

Serves 2
Prep Time: 5 minutes + freezing

1 ripe nectarine
4 scoops of your favorite vanilla ice cream
2 tablespoons extra-virgin olive oil
Zest of ½ lemon
1 teaspoon sea salt

Freeze the nectarine for 6 hours, or until completely frozen.

When ready to serve, place two scoops of ice cream into a bowl. Using a fine grater, grate the nectarine over each bowl.

Drizzle with the olive oil, then add the lemon zest and finish with a good pinch of salt. Serve.

Thai mango and coconut rice

This dish is inspired by my travels to Thailand. I remember first eating it and being totally blown away by how delicious this sticky rice is. You can have it for breakfast, but I love eating it as an ending to a special meal. Try to buy Pakistani mangos, as they are so juicy and sweet.

Serves 2
Prep Time: 10 minutes + overnight soaking
Cook Time: 30 minutes

1 cup (200 g) dry glutinous rice
1 cup (240 ml) full-fat coconut milk
3¼ tablespoons granulated sugar
Salt

FOR THE SAUCE
⅔ cup (160 ml) full-fat coconut milk
3 tablespoons granulated sugar
1 teaspoon cornstarch
Zest and juice of 1 lime

FOR SERVING
1 very ripe mango, preferably Pakistani or Indian, peeled and sliced into long strips
Toasted coconut, for topping
1 tablespoon toasted sesame seeds
Lime wedges

Add the rice to a strainer and rinse under cold running water to remove the excess starch until the water is almost running clear. Tip into a large bowl, cover with water, and let soak overnight for at least 8 hours.

The next day, drain the water from the rice. Line a bamboo steamer basket or steamer with baking parchment and tip in the rice. Set the steamer over a saucepan of simmering water and steam for 20 minutes, topping off the water if necessary. If you have a rice cooker, this works, too.

When the rice is cooked, pour the coconut milk into a medium pan and place it over medium to high heat. Add the sugar and a good pinch of salt.

Add the rice to the coconut milk pan and reduce the heat to low. Cook for 4 minutes, then remove from the heat and let stand.

For the sauce, bring the coconut milk and sugar to a boil in a small pan over medium heat, then reduce the heat to a simmer. In a small bowl, mix the cornstarch with the lime juice and zest and a little water until it is a smooth, thin consistency.

Add the cornstarch to the coconut milk and keep stirring until the sauce thickens. Cook for 3 minutes, or until thick and glossy. Pour into a pitcher.

Divide the rice between two bowls and serve with the mango, toasted coconut, and a sprinkle of toasted sesame seeds. Finish with a generous helping of sauce and lime wedges and serve.

Basque cheesecake

Serves 2
Prep Time: 10 minutes
Cook Time: 25 minutes

I first ate this unbelievable Spanish cheesecake when visiting San Sebastian. If you don't have small cake pans you can use 11-inch (28 cm) ramekins instead. Be careful when baking the cake as the center should still have jiggle, so once it is chilled, it will give you the perfect texture.

¾ cup (180 g) cream cheese, at room temperature
5 tablespoons superfine sugar
1 egg
⅓ cup (80 ml) heavy cream
1 teaspoon vanilla bean paste
1 tablespoon all-purpose flour

Preheat the oven to 400°F (200°C). Line two 11-inch (28 cm) cake pans or ramekins with wax paper. You want the paper to be pushed in and crinkled, as this gives the typical shape.

Whisk the cream cheese and sugar together in a stand mixer fitted with a whisk attachment until fluffy. Alternatively, use a bowl and a hand whisk. Whisk in the egg, then add the cream and vanilla bean paste and whisk until everything is combined. Whisk in the flour until the mixture is smooth and thickened.

Divide the batter equally among the cake pans or ramekins. Place on a baking sheet and tap on the counter to remove any air bubbles. Bake on the top shelf of the oven until deeply golden but the center still jiggles, 25 minutes.

Remove the cake from the oven and let cool, then chill in the refrigerator for 2 hours, or overnight before serving.

SWEET MOMENTS FOR TWO

Almond and cherry clafoutis

Serves 2
Prep Time: 10 minutes
Cook Time: 25 minutes

A clafoutis is like a very light sponge almost baked in custard with perfectly juicy bursts of fruit. If cherries are not in season, then use blackberries, blueberries, chopped nectarines, or even stewed apples. Serve with a good spoonful of crème fraîche or cream.

5 tablespoons (70 g) salted butter, plus extra for greasing
2 tablespoons demerara sugar
Scant ½ cup (100 ml) whole milk
⅓ cup (80 ml) heavy cream
1 teaspoon vanilla bean paste
1 eggs
1 egg yolk
¼ cup (50 g) superfine sugar
Zest of 1 lemon
Scant ½ cup (40 g) ground almonds
4¾ tablespoons all-purpose flour
1¼ cups (200 g) pitted cherries
1 handful of slivered almonds
Confectioners' sugar, for dusting
Crème fraîche or heavy cream, for serving

Preheat the oven to 350°F (180°C). Grease a 6-inch (15 cm) ovenproof skillet or baking dish with butter and sprinkle over the demerara sugar so the pan is well coated.

Pour the milk into a medium saucepan, add the butter, cream, and vanilla bean paste and bring to a simmer. Add the whole egg, then add the egg yolk and superfine sugar and whisk with a hand whisk until light and fluffy.

Slowly pour the hot cream into the egg mix. Fold in the lemon zest, ground almonds, and flour.

Spread the cherries out into the bottom of the skillet or pan and pour over the batter. Sprinkle the slivered almonds over the top and bake in the oven until just set, 25 minutes.

Remove the pan from the oven and let cool slightly before dusting with confectioners' sugar. Serve with crème fraîche or cream.

SWEET MOMENTS FOR TWO

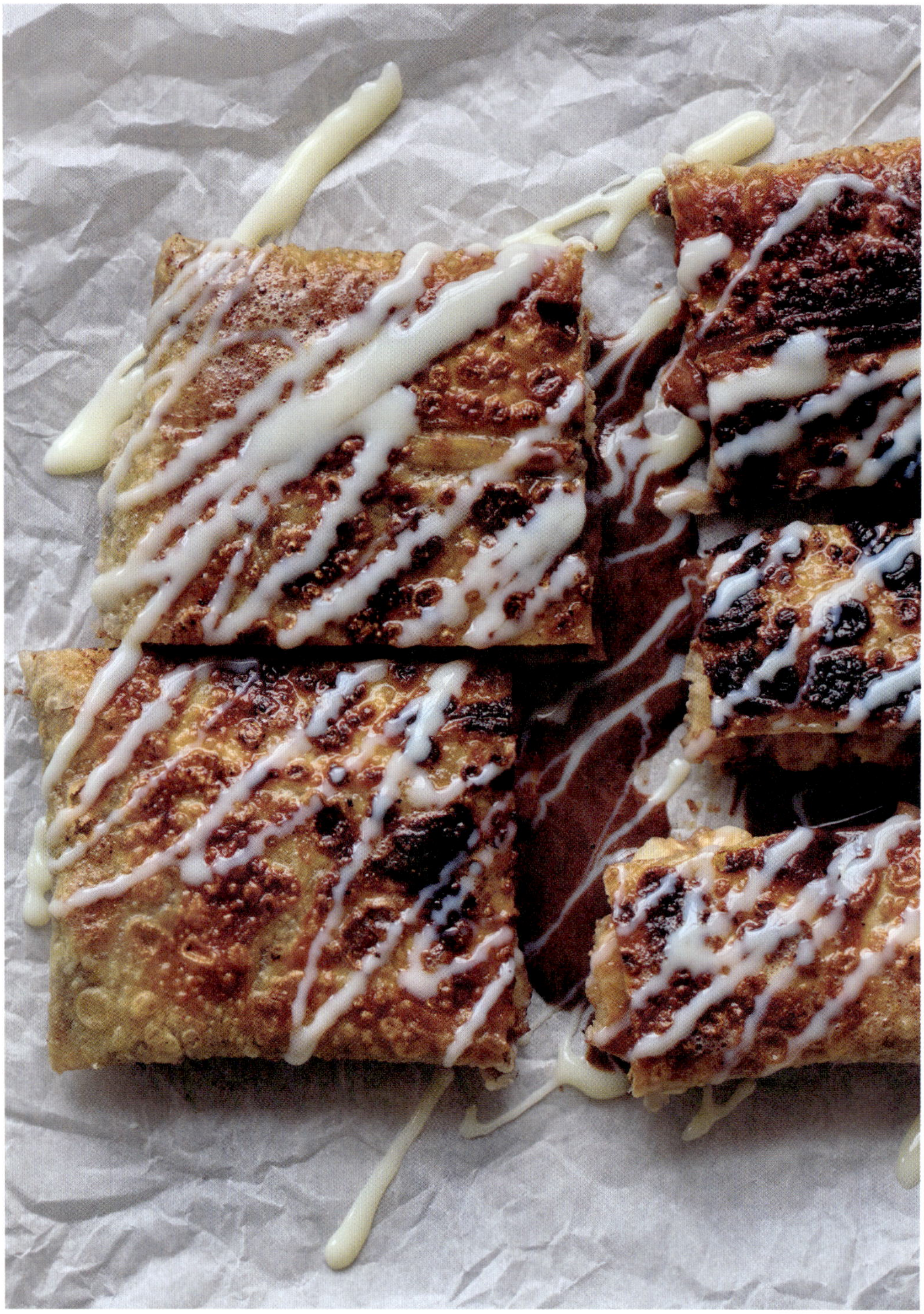

Crispy Thai banana roti

Serves 2
Prep Time: 5 minutes
Cook Time: 4 minutes

These crispy yet chewy pancakes are a riff on a street food staple in Thailand. I make them using store-bought phyllo for ease. I could definitely eat a whole roti myself, but this one is perfect for sharing. There is no need to be too neat with the folds; you just want to make sure the chocolate filling won't leak out when frying them.

1 large egg
¼ cup (60 ml) heavy cream
3 tablespoons chocolate hazelnut spread
2 tablespoons condensed milk, plus extra for drizzling
1 good pinch of salt
4 sheets of phyllo pastry
1 large banana, peeled and sliced
¼ cup (60 g) ghee, for frying

In a small bowl, whisk the egg and 2 tablespoons of the cream together until well mixed.

In a separate bowl, mix the hazelnut spread, the remaining cream, condensed milk, and salt together until combined.

Lay a sheet of phyllo pastry on a clean counter and brush with the egg mix. Add another sheet of phyllo on top and cover again. Repeat with the remaining sheets of phyllo.

Add the chocolate mix to the middle of the pastry and top with an even layer of banana slices. Fold the sides in, covering the banana and creating a square envelope.

Place the ghee in a heavy skillet and place over medium heat. When the ghee is very hot, add the roti and, using a spatula, press down and fry until crisp and dark spots appear, 2 minutes. Flip the roti over and fry for another 2 minutes.

Remove the roti from the pan, slice into eight pieces, drizzle with condensed milk, and serve.

COC

DREAMS

KTAILS

AND

My whiskey sour

Makes: 2
Prep Time: 1 minute

3½ ounces (100 ml) good-quality whiskey
Ice cubes
3½ tablespoons lemon juice
3½ tablespoons maple syrup
1 tablespoon maraschino liquid
Scant ½ cup (100 ml) chickpea water or 1 egg white
2 maraschino cherries
4 dashes of bitters

Chickpea water is the liquid from a can of chickpeas. You can also use an egg white if you prefer, but I find egg whites sometimes a little too thick. What's not to love here? A sharp, smooth, sweet, and decadent drink.

Pour the whiskey into a cocktail shaker and half-fill with ice. Add the lemon juice, maple syrup, maraschino liquid, and chickpea water or egg white. Attach the lid and vigorously shake for 4 seconds. You want the chickpea liquid to foam.

Pour the sour through a cocktail strainer into two short glasses of your choice. Top each with a cherry and two dashes of bitters.

Tangerine citrustini

Makes: 2
Prep Time: 12 minutes

8 tangerines, halved
Juice of ½ lemon
Ice cubes
1¾ ounces (50 ml) Vermouth Rosso
3½ ounces (100 ml) vodka or gin
2 leaves from the tangerines, for garnish (optional)

When winter citrus is at its best, this drink feels like one of those perfect cocktails for me. A little sweet yet fresh tangerine is really fragrant. If you can't get tangerines, clementines, satsumas, and even blood oranges work just as well.

Freeze two coupe glasses 10 minutes before serving.

Squeeze the tangerine juice into a pitcher and add the lemon juice. Fill a cocktail shaker with ice and pour in the tangerine juice. Add the vermouth and vodka and shake vigorously until the outside is frosty.

Pour into the chilled glasses and garnish with a tangerine leaf, if desired.

COCKTAILS AND DREAMS 163

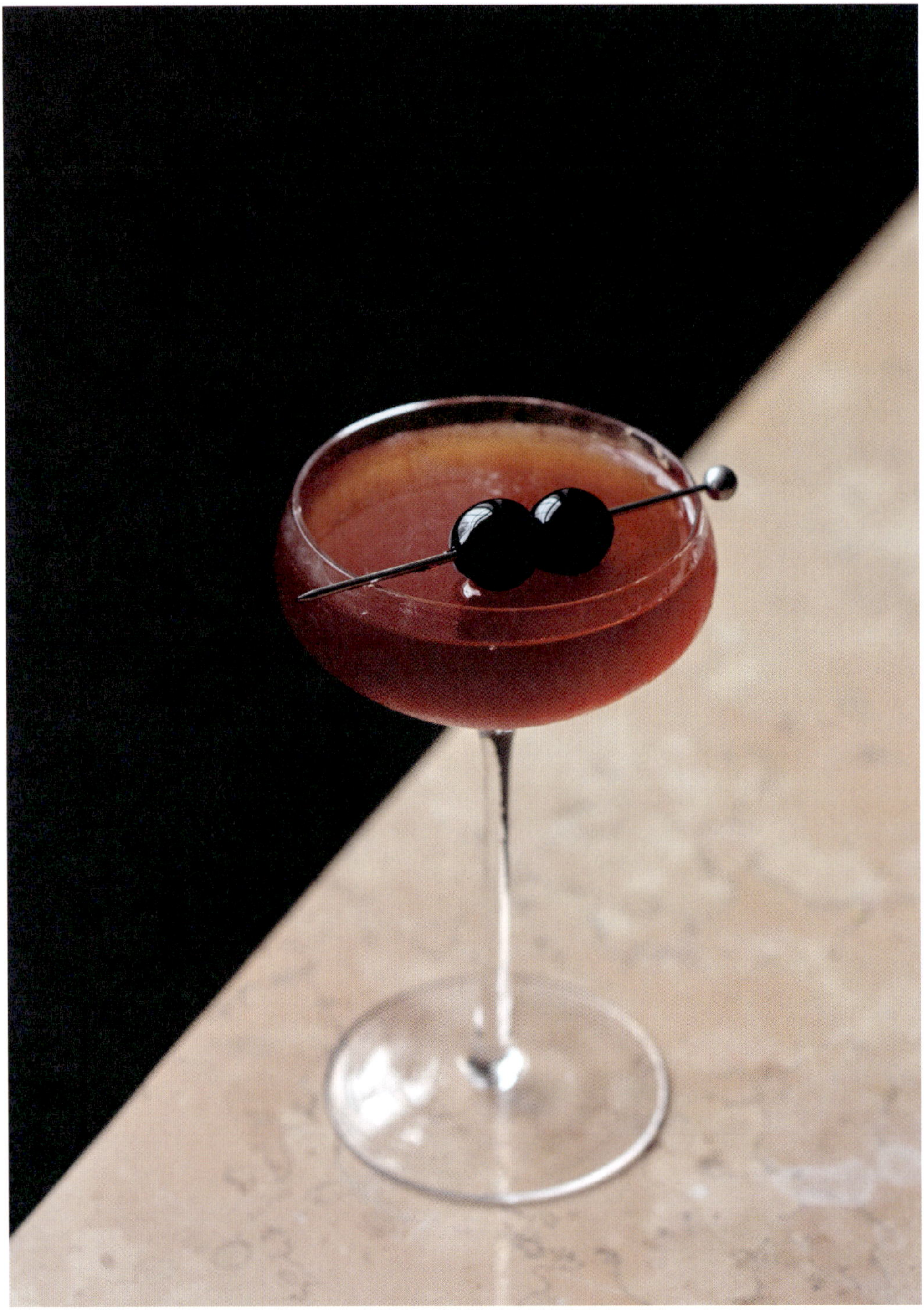

Dr. Pepper-style sweet delight

Makes: 2
Prep Time: 12 minutes

This cocktail has a sweet, almond, and cherry flavor, which is so good. Make sure you source maraschino cherries and not the bright red cocktail ones.

1 tablespoon maraschino liquid
6 maraschino cherries
1¾ ounces (50 ml) Disaronno
3½ ounces (100 ml) vodka
1 teaspoon lemon juice
Ice cubes

Freeze two coupe glasses 10 minutes before serving.

Add the maraschino liquid, two of the cherries, the Disaronno, vodka, and lemon juice to a shaker. Fill with ice, attach the lid, and shake vigorously until the outside is frosty.

Pour the drink through a cocktail strainer into the chilled glasses and top with two cherries.

COCKTAILS AND DREAMS

Vermouth spritz

Makes: 2
Prep Time: 2 minutes

Ice cubes
3½ ounces (100 ml) vermouth
7 ounces (200 ml) soda water
2 grapefruit wedges, for garnish
2 green olives, for garnish

A vermouth spritz is the ideal refreshing aperitif to every meal. In my opinion, it feels light and refreshing yet easy. I love Vermouth and always try to buy a good-quality one, but try and see what you like.

Fill two glasses with ice. Pour over the vermouth and top with the soda. Garnish with a grapefruit wedge and a green olive.

A perfect negroni

Makes: 2
Prep Time: 5 minutes

1 orange
Ice cubes, plus 2 large ice cubes, for serving
1¾ ounces (50 ml) gin
1¾ ounces (50 ml) sweet vermouth
1¾ ounces (50 ml) Campari

The perfect negroni can whisk me back to sitting in a square in Italy, watching the world go by. This potent cocktail always delivers a punch. I love a little fresh orange juice in mine, which is not traditional, but try it and see.

Using a vegetable peeler, peel two long strips of orange skin. Cut the strips into 4-inch (10 cm) long slices, trim the sides, then slice each end on an angle.

Add plenty of ice to a pitcher or cocktail mixing glass and pour over the gin, vermouth, and Campari. Halve the orange and squeeze in about 2 tablespoons of juice. Using a cocktail spoon or a long spoon, stir in a circular motion until the liquid is chilled.

Add a large ice cube to two short glasses and pour the negroni through a cocktail strainer into the glasses. Twist in the orange peel and serve.

COCKTAILS AND DREAMS

A dirty banana

Makes: 2
Prep Time: 5 minutes

I first drank this tropical smoothie-type cocktail in Cuba. The creamy frozen banana and coffee combination is so good and it is also perfect post-meal instead of a dessert. If you don't have any frozen bananas, just add a little extra ice.

4 ounces (120 ml) light gold rum
1¾ ounces (50 ml) coffee liqueur, such as Kahlua
2 ounces (60 ml) banana liqueur
¼ cup (60 ml) half and half
2 frozen bananas
1 large handful of ice cubes
2 banana slices, for garnish

Blend the rum, coffee liqueur, banana liqueur, half and half, frozen bananas, and ice in a blender until smooth and creamy. Pour into two glasses of choice and garnish with a banana slice.

Dirtiest martini

Makes: 2
Prep Time: 2 minutes

For me, there is no classier drink than a dirty martini. It is a cocktail with a lot of punch, so if you like a sweeter drink, this might not be your bag. With any cocktail, the quality of the ingredients is important, so try to find Perelló green olives if you can as they will make a difference to the drink.

Ice cubes
3½ ounces (100 ml) vodka
1¼ ounces (50 ml) dry vermouth
2 tablespoons olive brine from Perelló canned olives
Squeeze of lemon juice, plus 2 strips of lemon peel, for garnish
2 Perelló green olives, for garnish

Freeze two coupe glasses for 10 minutes before serving.

Half-fill a cocktail shaker with ice and add the vodka, vermouth, olive brine, and squeeze of lemon juice. Attach the lid and shake vigorously for 20 seconds, or until the shaker is frosty to the touch.

Strain the martini through a cocktail strainer into the chilled glasses. and garnish with a lemon peel twist and an olive.

Frozen coconut pineapple slush

Makes: 2
Prep Time: 5 minutes

When pineapples are in season and at their best, I spend time chopping and freezing them so I can quickly whip up this tropical delight on a hot summer's day. You can also buy frozen pineapple. Serve with a straw for a tropical vibe.

2 cups (330 g) frozen pineapple chunks
3½ ounces (100 ml) coconut cream
7 ounces (200 ml) pineapple juice
Juice of 1 lime
4 ounces (120 ml) coconut rum
1 handful of ice cubes
4 pineapple leaves, for garnish (optional)

Blend the pineapple chunks, coconut cream, pineapple juice, lime juice, rum, and ice in a high-speed blender until smooth and slushy.

Pour into two tall glasses and garnish with a pineapple leaves, if desired.

COCKTAILS AND DREAMS

Summer green garden

Makes: 2
Prep Time: 12 minutes

1 cucumber
1 apple
3½ ounces (100 ml) gin
2 tablespoons store-bought simple syrup
1¾ ounces (50 ml) lime juice
Ice cubes

If you do not have a juicer, buy good-quality cloudy apple juice, then blend the cucumber and strain the liquid. You can keep the cucumber juice in the refrigerator for up to two days for when you want another.

Freeze two coupe glasses 10 minutes before serving. Peel two long strips of cucumber for the garnish and set aside.

Blend the cucumber and apple in a juicer, then pour ¾ cup (180 ml) of the liquid into a cocktail shaker. Add the gin, simple syrup, lime juice, and plenty of ice, attach the lid, and shake until the outside is icy cold.

Drape the cucumber slices around the inside of the chilled glasses and pour the liquid through a cocktail strainer into the glasses.

Spicy tequila picante

Makes: 2
Prep Time: 2 minutes

I think a spicy, smooth, zesty picante will always be my go-to cocktail. Make sure you buy good-quality tequila, as it makes all the difference. If you don't have Tajin salt, you can use sea salt or just omit salting the rim altogether. Cocktails are like your coffee order; make it how it suits you. If you want it zestier, add more lime, or if you want it slightly sweeter, then add more syrup.

3½ ounces (100 ml) tequila
1 cup (15 g) cilantro
2 jalapeños, sliced
Ice cubes
Juice of 2 limes, about 3 ounces (90 ml)
2 tablespoons agave syrup or maple syrup

FOR THE RIM
2 tablespoons Tajin salt
½ lime

Pour the tequila into a cocktail shaker, add the cilantro and jalapeños, setting aside two slices for the garnish. Use a muddler or rolling pin to give it a good muddle.

To rim the glasses, spread the salt out onto a plate. Rub the lime around two short glasses of your choice, then press the rim of each glass into the salt until the rim is coated. Add a couple of large ice cubes to each glass.

Add the lime juice and agave syrup to the shaker and fill it with ice. Attach the lid and shake vigorously for about 15 seconds.

Pour the drink through a cocktail strainer into the glasses. Top with the reserved jalapeño slices and serve.

COCKTAILS AND DREAMS

Clarified grapefruit margarita

Makes: 24-ounce (720 ml) bottle
Prep Time: 15 minutes

I first drank this margarita during lockdown. A local East London bar had started bottling and selling it. Even though this is a little more time-consuming than my other drinks, the reward is that the bottle will last a year in the refrigerator. It is perfect to make and then keep for when you want a fancy drink. It is also great to take to a barbecue or picnic.

8 ounces (240 ml) fresh grapefruit juice
4 ounces (120 ml) fresh lime juice
8 ounces (240 ml) triple sec
½ cup (120 ml) agave syrup
16 ounces (480 ml) tequila
1 large pinch of salt
¾ cup (180 ml) whole milk
Ice cubes, for serving

Add the grapefruit juice, lime juice, triple sec, agave syrup, tequila, and salt to a large bowl and whisk well until combined.

Add the milk and let stand for a few hours. The milk will curdle.

Line a strainer with a cheesecloth or a paper coffee filter and set the strainer over a clean bowl or large pitcher. Pour the mix through the strainer, catching the clear liquid in the bowl.

Discard the cheesecloth and repeat the straining with new cheesecloth or paper coffee filter until the liquid is clear.

Pour into a sterilized bottle and chill. When ready to drink, pour over a large ice cube.

COCKTAILS AND DREAMS 175

THE
ART
SNACKING

OF
COCKTAIL

Buttered spiced toasted nuts

Serves: 2
Prep Time: 5 minutes
Cook Time: 5 minutes

This lightly caramelized salty and sweet nut mix is great while sipping a cool cocktail. You can add whatever woody herbs you like and play around with the spices. Just be careful when handling the hot sugar as it can burn very easily.

2 tablespoons butter
2 cups (250 g) unsalted mixed nuts, such as pecans, almonds, cashews, and macadamias
2 tablespoons soft light brown sugar
2 tablespoons coarsely chopped rosemary
1 teaspoon sweet smoked paprika
¼ teaspoon red pepper flakes
1 teaspoon flaky sea salt

Melt the butter in a large skillet over medium heat and add the nuts. Fry, stirring frequently, until the nuts and butter are golden. Tip into a heatproof bowl and set aside.

Melt the sugar in a saucepan over medium heat until starting to caramelize. Add the rosemary and fry for 1 minute. Add the paprika and red pepper flakes, then carefully pour over the nuts. Toss with a wooden spoon, then tip out onto a baking sheet to cool. Sprinkle over the salt, then break up when cooled.

Elevated potato chips

Serves: 2
Prep Time: 5 minutes

This recipe was inspired by my sister, who used to just dip potato chips into a bowl of mayonnaise for her dinner. You can use any potato chip flavor you like. I just love the sharp salty and vinegary vibes contrasting with the creamy mayonnaise.

1 (10-ounce / 280 g) bag of thin salt and vinegar potato chips of your choice
2 tablespoons kewpie mayonnaise
1 teaspoon Tajin salt
3 dashes of Tabasco sauce
6 pickled jalapeños

Tip the potato chips into a bowl. Squeeze over the mayonnaise, then top with the salt, Tabasco, and chiles. Serve.

THE ART OF COCKTAIL SNACKING

Whipped butter and salted radishes

Serves: 2
Prep Time: 10 minutes

⅔ sticks (150 g) butter, at room temperature
3½ tablespoons buttermilk or milk
1 large pinch of flaky sea salt, plus extra for serving
1 bunch of leafy radishes

This butter whips up like a cloud. You can spread it on almost anything, but I love the contrast of the salty butter and peppery radishes.

Add the butter to a stand mixer fitted with a whisk attachment and whisk the butter on high speed for 5 minutes.

Turn the machine off, and scrape down the sides with a spatula. Reduce the speed to low and pour in the buttermilk. Once combined, turn the mixer back up to high and whisk until the mixture is pale and fluffy, 5 to 7 minutes.

Sprinkle in the sea salt, fold in, then pile into a small bowl. Serve with the radishes and a little extra flaky salt.

Stuffed queen olives with blue cheese

Makes: 10
Prep Time: 10 minutes

2 tablespoons whole cream cheese
1 ounce (30 g) blue cheese
1 teaspoon chopped thyme leaves
1 pinch of red pepper flakes
Zest of ½ lemon
10 large pitted queen olives
1 teaspoon runny honey

If I'm preparing a special meal for my husband, I will make these and serve them with the Dirtiest Martini on page 169 as an appetizer. The combination of green olives and blue cheese is divine but just try not to fill up on them.

Add the cream cheese, blue cheese, thyme, red pepper flakes, and lemon zest to a large bowl and mix well until smooth.

Spoon or pipe into the olives and serve or chill in the refrigerator. When ready to serve, drizzle the olives with honey.

Anchovies and charred bread

Makes: 10
Prep Time: 10 minutes
Cook Time: 4 minutes

2 tablespoons olive oil
2 slices sourdough bread
1 garlic clove, peeled but left whole
2 tablespoons cold butter
1 (1.7-ounce / 47.5 g) tin anchovy filets in olive oil

These charred, oily breads topped with anchovies and cold butter are perfect any time. Make sure to buy the best tinned anchovies you can find, and always purchase them in olive oil.

Place a griddle or stovetop grill pan over high heat.

Drizzle the olive oil over the sourdough. Once the griddle is hot, char the bread on each side until you have dark charred lines, 2 minutes on each side. Remove from the heat and rub the garlic over each toast.

Slice the bread into triangles and let cool slightly. Slice slithers of the cold butter and top each triangle with butter and an anchovy, then serve. You can also serve everything separately and make your own together.

Mackerel pâte on toast

Serves: 2
Prep Time: 10 minutes

2 cured smoked mackerel filets, skinned
¼ cup (60 g) cream cheese
¼ cup (60 g) crème fraîche
2 teaspoons creamed horseradish
4 slices of rye bread
Juice of ½ lemon
1 small handful of dill
8 caper berries
Salt and pepper

Something about a pâte always feels so sophisticated to me and this can be prepared in minutes. I love to pair it with my Vermouth Spritz (see page 166). I have also been known to make one too many and happily eat it for dinner and even non-fish lovers will love this pâte.

Flake half the mackerel into a food processor, add the cream cheese, crème fraîche, and horseradish, and blitz until smooth.

Toast the rye bread.

Season the pâte with salt and pepper and add the lemon juice. Fold through the reserved mackerel, then serve on the rye toasts, garnished with dill and caper berries.

THE ART OF COCKTAIL SNACKING 183

Comté and thyme cheese straws

Makes: 12
Prep Time: 10 minutes
Cook Time: 20 minutes

1 (11-ounce / 320 g) all-butter puff pastry sheet
2 tablespoons all-purpose flour
1 egg, whisked
2 tablespoons Dijon mustard
1 small bunch of thyme, leaves picked
2 green chiles, chopped (optional)
¾ cup (80 g) grated Comté
1 tablespoon sesame seeds
Salt and pepper

I don't think I have ever met anyone who isn't into oozy cheese and flaky buttery pastry. These twists are so satisfying to make, and once you have made your own you'll never buy store-bought again.

Preheat the oven to 350°F (180°C). Line a large baking sheet with baking parchment.

Unroll the pastry sheet out onto a clean counter. Sprinkle the flour on top of the pastry sheet and flip the sheet over. Using a rolling pin, roll the sheet out to 10 by 12 inches (25 by 30 cm), moving the sheet of pastry as you go so it doesn't stick to the counter.

Brush a layer of egg across the whole pastry, then brush the mustard over. Sprinkle over the thyme leaves and chiles, if using, followed by the cheese, setting aside a handful for the top.

Fold the sheet in half like folding a book in half, then roll the sheet out to about 8 by 8 inches (20 by 20 cm). It doesn't have to be exact as you just want to squash the layers together well.

Using a knife or a pizza cutter, cut the sheet into 12 equal long strips, then gently twist the strips.

Lay each finished twist on the lined baking sheet and brush with the remaining egg, the sesame seeds, and the reserved cheese. Season with salt and pepper and bake until golden and crisp, 20 minutes. Let cool for 5 minutes, then serve.

Prosciutto-wrapped figs with goat cheese

Jammy roasted figs stuffed with gooey roasted goat cheese and wrapped in prosciutto are so simple yet delicious. I like to serve mine straight out of the oven.

Serves: 2
Prep Time: 10 minutes
Cook Time: 20 minutes

6 whole figs
Scant ½ cup (100 g) soft goat cheese
1 garlic clove, sliced lengthwise
6 basil leaves
3 sheets of prosciutto, sliced in half lengthwise
1 tablespoon olive oil
1 teaspoon red wine vinegar
1 tablespoon honey
1 teaspoon fennel seeds
Salt and pepper
Crispbread or crackers, for serving

Preheat the oven to 375°F (190°C).

Cut a cross in each fig and fill with an equal amount of goat cheese. Top with a garlic clove and a basil leaf, then loosely wrap the fig in the prosciutto and place in a small ovenproof dish.

Drizzle over the olive oil, vinegar, and honey. Season with salt, fennel seeds, and pepper, and bake until the cheese and figs are oozy and jammy, 20 minutes.

Serve with crispbread.

Stuffed fried jalapeños

I'm a huge fan of spicy food, so these crispy, deep-fried stuffed jalapeños are so addictive. I love having them with a Dr. Pepper-Style Sweet Delight (see page 165). They are best eaten immediately so they are crispy. I like to keep the stems on the chiles as they are easier to handle, but it is up to you.

THE ART OF COCKTAIL SNACKING

Serves: 2
Prep Time: 15 minutes
Cook Time: 10 minutes

Sunflower or peanut oil, for deep-frying
6 large jalapeños
¼ cup (60 g) whole cream cheese
1 tablespoon chopped cilantro
½ cup (50 g) grated mozzarella
1 teaspoon sweet smoked paprika
Zest and juice of 1 lime
1¼ cups (100 g) dried breadcrumbs
¾ cup (100 g) all-purpose flour
1 tablespoon garlic powder
1 teaspoon onion powder
2 eggs
Salt and pepper
1 lime, cut into wedges, for serving

Soak 12 wooden toothpicks in a bowl of water for at least 30 minutes to prevent them burning during cooking.

When ready to cook, heat enough oil for deep-frying in a large, deep pot or deep-fryer over medium heat until the oil reaches 338°F to 394°F (170°C to 200°C) on a thermometer. Line a plate with paper towels.

Slice the tops off the jalapeños and set aside. Using a teaspoon, scoop out the seeds and discard. Set aside.

For the filling, mix the cream cheese, cilantro, mozzarella, paprika, and lime zest and juice together in a bowl until well combined. Season to taste with salt.

Using a pastry bag or, simply spoon the mixture into the jalapeños until filled, then using the soaked toothpicks, skewer the lid on the diagonal from each side so they are secure.

Spread the breadcrumbs out a plate. Spread the flour out on another plate. Season with salt and pepper, then mix in the garlic and onion powder. Whisk the eggs in a wide bowl.

Working with one pepper at a time, roll the pepper in the flour, making sure it is evenly coated, then roll the pepper in the egg, followed by the breadcrumbs until evenly coated. Set aside and continue until all the peppers are coated. Repeat the coating so the peppers have a really good covering.

Once the oil is hot, carefully add a few peppers at a time, making sure not to overcrowd the pot, and deep-fry until golden brown and crisp, 4 to 5 minutes. Using a slotted spoon, remove the peppers from the oil and drain on the lined plate. Sprinkle with salt and serve with lime wedges.

INDEX

A perfect negroni 166
acorn squash: Caramelized squash with whipped feta 65
A dirty banana 168
Almond and cherry clafoutis 156
Anchovies and charred bread 182
avocado: Lemongrass fish cakes with avocado and carrot salad 37
  Sesame-crusted seared tuna with a crispy garlic and chile salad 88
  Spicy tuna tostadas with jalapeño avocado guacamole 18

Baked cod with lemon, cannellini beans, and a dill and pickle sauce 104
Baked rice and herb salad 123
Baked salmon with crispy capers and speedy green aioli 12
Banana, rum, and lime tarte tatin 142
bananas: A dirty banana 168
  Banana, rum, and lime tarte tatin 142
  Crispy Thai banana roti 159
Basque cheesecake 154
beans: Baked cod with lemon, cannellini beans, and a dill and pickle sauce 104
  Niçoise salad with crispy green beans 52
  Spicy black bean stew 120
beef: Beef wellington with horseradish spinach 80
  My perfect red wine ragù 111
  Steak and chimichurri with garlic potatoes 46
Beef wellington with horseradish spinach 80
bell peppers: Harissa charred vegetables with flatbread and spiked yogurt 31
  Spiced green risotto 84

Brussels sprouts: Whipped tahini and Brussels sprout salad 71
Butter: Buttered spiced toasted nuts 178
  One-pan roast chicken with lemon and herb butter and roasted shallots 114
  Pistachio and ricotta gnudi with butter and sage sauce 106
  Spinach, feta, and herb pie with labneh and Turkish chile butter 72
  Steak and chimichurri with garlic potatoes 46
  Warm brown butter cookie cake with ice cream 139
  Whipped butter and salted radishes 180
Buttered spiced toasted nuts 178

capers: Baked salmon with crispy capers and speedy green aioli 12
  Confit tomato and caper tart with Parmesan 98
  My perfect Caesar 44
  Pan pizza 66
Caramelized squash with whipped feta 65
carrots: Crispy pork banh mi 130
  Lemongrass fish cakes with avocado and carrot salad 37
  My perfect red wine ragù 111
Celebration chocolate Guinness cake 148
celery root: Crispy pork chops with roasted grapes and celery root mash 94
cheese: Basque cheesecake 154
  Caramelized squash with whipped feta 65
  Comté and thyme cheese straws 184

Confit tomato and caper tart with Parmesan 98
Creamy cashew green pasta 32
Crispy chicken cutlets with olive, tomato, nectarine, and mozzarella salad 102
Crispy fried whole eggplant with tomato sauce 60
Crispy gnocchi with corn, ricotta, and spinach 28
Crispy pork belly with fennel and potato gratin 128
Decadent lasagna 112
Farinata-style pancakes, jarred vegetable salad, and lemon zest ricotta 38
Fried lemon spaghetti 25
Greek shrimp and orzo bake 100
Lady and the tramp spaghetti and meatballs with a spiced tomato sauce 86
Lebanese chopped salad 40
Olive, orzo, and feta bake 57
Pan pizza 66
Pasta alla norma with crispy capers and ricotta salata 50
Pistachio and ricotta gnudi with butter and sage sauce 106
Pork sausage and fennel tagliatelle 93
Prosciutto-wrapped figs with goat cheese 185
Spiced green risotto 84
Spicy makhani paneer curry and parathas 121
Spinach, feta, and herb pie with labneh and Turkish chile butter 72
Steak and chimichurri with garlic potatoes 46
Stuffed fried jalapeños 186
Stuffed queen olives with blue cheese 181

Vodka and gochujang pasta 74
Watermelon, feta, and za'atar salad 68
cherries: Almond and cherry clafoutis 156
chicken: Chinese poached chicken with ginger dipping oil and steamed rice 58
   Crispy chicken cutlets with olive, tomato, nectarine, and mozzarella salad 102
   My perfect Caesar 44
   One-pan roast chicken with lemon and herb butter and roasted shallots 114
   Roast chicken and ricotta tortellini in broth 116
   Thai basil and chicken stir-fry with a crispy egg 26
   Whipped tahini and Brussels sprout salad 71
Chinese poached chicken with ginger dipping oil and steamed rice 58
chocolate: Celebration chocolate Guinness cake 148
   Earl Grey chocolate pudding 141
   Miso and dark chocolate freezer cookies 146
   My heavenly Calvados tiramisu 134
Clarified grapefruit margarita 174
cocktails: A dirty banana 168
   A perfect negroni 166
   Clarified grapefruit margarita 174
   Dirtiest martini 169
   Dr. Pepper-style sweet delight 165
   Frozen coconut pineapple slush 170
   My whiskey sour 162
   Spicy tequila picante 173
   Summer green garden 172
   Tangerine citrustini 162
   Vermouth spritz 166
coconut: Frozen coconut pineapple slush 170
   Thai mango and coconut rice 152
coffee: My heavenly Calvados tiramisu 134

Comté and thyme cheese straws 184
Confit tomato and caper tart with Parmesan 98
corn: Corn chowder and seared scallops 90
   Crispy gnocchi with corn, ricotta, and spinach 28
Corn chowder and seared scallops 90
Creamy cashew green pasta 32
Crispy chicken cutlets with olive, tomato, nectarine, and mozzarella salad 102
Crispy fried whole eggplant with tomato sauce 60
Crispy gnocchi with corn, ricotta, and spinach 28
Crispy pork banh mi 130
Crispy pork belly with fennel and potato gratin 128
Crispy pork chops with roasted grapes and celery root mash 94
Crispy Thai banana roti 159
Cucumber: Spicy crispy gyoza with smashed cucumber salad 124

Decadent lasagna 112
Dirtiest martini 169
Dr. Pepper-style sweet delight 165

Earl Grey chocolate pudding 141
eggplant: Crispy fried whole eggplant with tomato sauce 60
   Harissa charred vegetables with flatbread and spiked yogurt 31
   Pasta alla norma with crispy capers and ricotta salata 50
eggs: Nasi lemak–coconut rice with sambal and a crispy egg 54
   Shortcut miso ramen 20
   Thai basil and chicken stir-fry with a crispy egg 26
Elevated potato chips 178

Farinata-style pancakes, jarred vegetable salad, and lemon zest ricotta 38

fennel: Crispy pork belly with fennel and potato gratin 128
   Pasta with fennel, tuna, and Pernod 96
   Pork sausage and fennel tagliatelle 93
figs: Prosciutto-wrapped figs with goat cheese 185
fish: Anchovies and charred bread 182
   Baked cod with lemon, cannellini beans, and a dill and pickle sauce 104
   Baked salmon with crispy capers and speedy green aioli 12
   Lemongrass fish cakes with avocado and carrot salad 37
   Mackerel pâte on toast 182
   My perfect Caesar 44
   Nasi lemak–coconut rice with sambal and a crispy egg 54
   Niçoise salad with crispy green beans 52
   Pan pizza 66
   Pasta with fennel, tuna, and Pernod 96
   Salmon tikka skewers with a cilantro marinade 34
   Sesame-crusted seared tuna with a crispy garlic and chile salad 88
   Spicy tuna tostadas with jalapeño guacamole 18
   Steamed whole fish finished with a sizzling scallion oil 79
   The perfect smoked salmon omelet with chive and dill crème fraîche 23
Fried lemon spaghetti 25
Frozen coconut pineapple slush 170
Grated frozen nectarine with olive oil and salt over ice cream 151

ginger: Chinese poached chicken with ginger dipping oil and steamed rice 58
gnocchi: Crispy gnocchi with corn, ricotta, and spinach 28
grapes: Crispy pork chops with

INDEX   189

roasted grapes and celery root mash 94
Greek shrimp and orzo bake 100
Gyoza in broth with chili crisp and greens 126
gyozas: Gyoza in broth with chili crisp and greens 126
  Spicy crispy gyoza with smashed cucumber salad 124

Harissa charred vegetables with flatbread and spiked yogurt 31

jalapeños: Stuffed fried jalapeños 186

kohlrabi: Schnitzel and kohlrabi slaw 48

Lady and the tramp spaghetti and meatballs with a spiced tomato sauce 86
Lebanese chopped salad 40
Lemongrass fish cakes with avocado and carrot salad 37

Mackerel pâte on toast 182
mango: Thai mango and coconut rice 152
mayonnaise: Baked salmon with crispy capers and speedy green aioli 12
  Vegetable fritti with 'nduja aioli 62
miso: Miso and dark chocolate freezer cookies 146
Miso and dark chocolate freezer cookies 146
My carnitas tacos 119
My heavenly Calvados tiramisu 134
My perfect Caesar 44
My perfect red wine ragù 111
My whiskey sour 162
mushrooms: Beef wellington with horseradish spinach 80

Nasi lemak—coconut rice with sambal and a crispy egg 54
nectarines: Crispy chicken cutlets with olive, tomato, nectarine, and mozzarella salad 102
  Frozen nectarine grated with olive oil and salt ice cream 151
Niçoise salad with crispy green beans 52
noodles: Sesame sticky noodles 15
  Shortcut miso ramen 20
nuts: Almond and cherry clafoutis 156
  Buttered spiced toasted nuts 178
  Caramelized squash with whipped feta 65
  Creamy cashew green pasta 32
  Orange blossom and lemon granita 144
  Pistachio and ricotta gnudi with butter and sage sauce 106
  Sesame-crusted seared tuna with a crispy garlic and chile salad 88
  Sesame sticky noodles 15
  Spiced green risotto 84
  Whipped tahini and Brussels sprout salad 71

Olive, orzo, and feta bake 57
olives: Crispy chicken cutlets with olive, tomato, nectarine, and mozzarella salad 102
  Niçoise salad with crispy green beans 52
  Olive, orzo, and feta bake 57
  Stuffed queen olives with blue cheese 181
  Watermelon, feta, and za'atar salad 68
One-pan roast chicken with lemon and herb butter and roasted shallots 114
Orange blossom and lemon granita 144

Pan pizza 66
pasta: Creamy cashew green pasta 32
  Decadent lasagna 112
  Fried lemon spaghetti 25
  Greek shrimp and orzo bake 100
  Lady and the tramp spaghetti and meatballs with a spiced tomato sauce 86
  My perfect red wine ragù 111
  Olive, orzo, and feta bake 57
  Pasta alla norma with crispy capers and ricotta salata 50
  Pasta alla vongole 82
  Pasta with fennel, tuna, and Pernod 96
  Pork sausage and fennel tagliatelle 93
  Roast chicken and ricotta tortellini in broth 116
  Vodka and gochujang pasta 74
Pasta alla norma with crispy capers and ricotta salata 50
Pasta alla vongole 82
Pasta with fennel, tuna, and Pernod 96
Pistachio and ricotta gnudi with butter and sage sauce 106
Plum upside-side cake with lemon zest 137
plums: Plum upside-side cake with lemon zest 137
pork: Beef wellington with horseradish spinach 80
  Corn chowder and seared scallops 90
  Crispy pork banh mi 130
  Crispy pork belly with braised fennel and potatoes 128
  Crispy pork chops with roasted grapes and celery root mash 94
  Lady and the tramp spaghetti and meatballs with a spiced tomato sauce 86
  My carnitas tacos 119
  My perfect red wine ragù 111
  Pork sausage and fennel tagliatelle 93
  Prosciutto-wrapped figs with goat cheese 185
  Schnitzel and kohlrabi slaw 48
  Spicy black bean stew 120
  Vegetable fritti with 'nduja aioli 62
Pork sausage and fennel tagliatelle 93

Potatoes: Crispy pork belly with fennel and potato gratin 128
   Elevated potato chips 178
   Niçoise salad with crispy green beans 52
   One-pan roast chicken with lemon and herb butter and roasted shallots 114
   Steak and chimichurri with garlic potatoes 46
Prosciutto-wrapped figs with goat cheese 185

radishes: Whipped butter and salted radishes 180
Red curry and coconut mussels 16
rice: Baked rice and herb salad 123
   Chinese poached chicken with ginger dipping oil and steamed rice 58
   Nasi lemak—coconut rice with sambal and a crispy egg 54
   Spiced green risotto 84
   Thai mango and coconut rice 152
Roast chicken and ricotta tortellini in broth 116

Salmon tikka skewers with a cilantro marinade 34
scallions: Gyoza in broth with chili crisp and greens 126
   Sesame-crusted seared tuna with a crispy garlic and chile salad 88
   Steamed whole fish finished with a sizzling scallion oil 79
Schnitzel and kohlrabi slaw 48
seafood: Corn chowder and seared scallops 90
   Greek shrimp and orzo bake 100
   Pasta alla vongole 82
   Red curry and coconut mussels 16
   Sesame-crusted seared tuna with a crispy garlic and chile salad 88
Sesame sticky noodles 15
Shortcut miso ramen 20
Spiced green risotto 84

Spicy black bean stew 120
Spicy crispy gyoza with smashed cucumber salad 124
Spicy makhani paneer curry and parathas 121
Spicy tequila picante 173
Spicy tuna tostadas with jalapeño avocado guacamole 18
spinach: Beef wellington with horseradish spinach 80
   Crispy gnocchi with corn, ricotta, and spinach 28
   Gyoza in broth with chili crisp and greens 126
   Spinach, feta, and herb pie with labneh and Turkish chile butter 72
Spinach, feta, and herb pie with labneh and Turkish chile butter 72
Steak and chimichurri with garlic potatoes 46
Steamed whole fish finished with a sizzling scallion oil 79
Stuffed fried jalapeños 186
Stuffed queen olives with blue cheese 181
Summer green garden 172

tahini: Whipped tahini and Brussels sprout salad 71
Tangerine citrustini 162
tofu: Earl Grey chocolate pudding 141
tomatoes: Baked rice and Indian herb salad 123
   Confit tomato and caper tart with Parmesan 98
   Crispy chicken cutlets with olive, tomato, nectarine, and mozzarella salad 102
   Crispy fried whole eggplant with tomato sauce 60
   Greek shrimp and orzo bake 100
   Lady and the tramp spaghetti and meatballs with a spiced tomato sauce 86
   Lebanese chopped salad 40
   My perfect red wine ragù 111

Niçoise salad with crispy green beans 52
Pan pizza 66
Pasta alla norma with crispy capers and ricotta salata 50
Pasta alla vongole 82
Vodka and gochujang pasta 74
Thai basil and chicken stir-fry with a crispy egg 26
Thai mango and coconut rice 152
The perfect smoked salmon omelet with chive and dill crème fraiche 23

Vegetable fritti with 'nduja aioli 62
Vermouth spritz 166
Vodka and gochujang pasta 74

watermelon: Watermelon, feta, and za'atar salad 68
Watermelon, feta, and za'atar salad 68
Warm brown butter cookie cake with ice cream 139
Whipped butter and salted radishes 180
Whipped tahini and Brussels sprout salad 71

yogurt: Harissa charred vegetables with flatbread and spiked yogurt 31
   My perfect Caesar 44
   Salmon tikka skewers with a cilantro marinade 34

zucchini: Harissa charred vegetables with flatbread and spiked yogurt 31

ACKNOWLEDGMENTS

I want to start by saying thank you to you, the reader—the person holding this book, the person flicking through it and making plans for all your meals ahead. Without you, this would be nothing. I can't wait to see what you cook and how it brings you all together. Thank you, Catie Ziller, for constantly pushing me and for continuously commissioning me to write about the things I love. Thanks to Jenny Wapner and her team for allowing me to create this book and for sharing your words of wisdom along the way. To my husband, Sebastian, thank you for being my rock in life, for trying every single recipe, and for giving me utterly honest feedback, even when I sometimes ignore it. Issy Croker, thank you for being the world's best photographer. Working with you all these years has been the best. Thank you to Narroway Studio for being the home that kept the shoot together. Thank you, Jo, for always being my right-hand man during the shoot, for bringing so much cheer and good vibes, and to the amazing Sunni for all your hard work. Thank you, Claire Rochford, for the brilliant design of this book and joining us on the journey. Kathy, thank you for all your help with my edits. I know it's not easy, but you do it effortlessly and always with a helping hand.

Hardie Grant North America

2912 Telegraph Ave
Berkeley, CA 94705
hardiegrant.com

Text © 2025 by Emily Ezekiel
Photographs © 2025 by Issy Croker
Illustrations © 2025 by Claire Rochford

All rights reserved. No part of this book may be reproduced in any form without written permission from the publisher.

Published in the United States by Hardie Grant North America, an imprint of Hardie Grant Publishing Pty Ltd.

Library of Congress Cataloging-in-Publication Data is available upon request
ISBN: 9781964786148
ISBN: (eBook) 9781964786155

Acquisitions Editor: Catie Ziller
Photographer: Issy Croker
Prop styling: Emily Ezekiel
Designer and illustrator: Claire Rochford
Copy Editor: Kathy Steer

Printed in China

FIRST EDITION

Hardie Grant
NORTH AMERICA